ARCHITECTURAL DESIGN

T0374498

GUEST-EDITED BY
ACHIM MENGES

MATERIAL COMPUTATION
HIGHER INTEGRATION IN MORPHOGENETIC DESIGN

02|2012

ARCHITECTURAL DESIGN
MARCH/APRIL 2012
ISSN 0003-8504

PROFILE NO 216
ISBN 978-0470-973301

IN THIS ISSUE

ARCHITECTURAL DESIGN

GUEST-EDITED BY
ACHIM MENGES

MATERIAL COMPUTATION: HIGHER INTEGRATION IN MORPHOGENETIC DESIGN

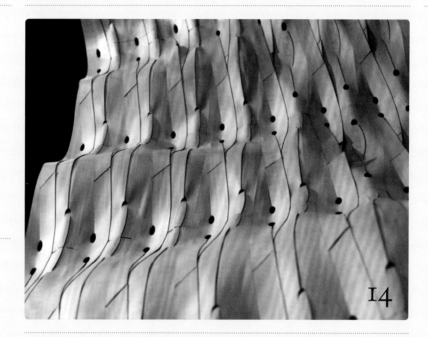

14

*A novel convergence of computation and materialisation
is about to arise, bringing the virtual processes of
computational design and the physical realisation of
architecture much closer together …*
— *Achim Menges*

44

68

ARCHITECTURAL DESIGN
MARCH/APRIL 2012
PROFILE NO 216

Editorial Offices
John Wiley & Sons
25 John Street
London
WC1N 2BS

T: +44 (0)20 8326 3800

Editor
Helen Castle

Managing Editor (Freelance)
Caroline Ellerby

Production Editor
Elizabeth Gongde

Prepress
Artmedia, London

Art Direction and Design
CHK Design:
Christian Küsters
Sophie Troppmair

Printed in Italy by Conti Tipocolor

Sponsorship/advertising
Faith Pidduck/Wayne Frost
T: +44 (0)1243 770254
E: fpidduck@wiley.co.uk

Subscribe to ᗐ

ᗐ is published bimonthly and is
available to purchase on both a
subscription basis and as individual
volumes at the following prices.

Prices
Individual copies: £22.99 / US$45
Mailing fees may apply

Annual Subscription Rates
Student: £75 / US$117 print only
Individual: £120 / US$189 print only
Institutional: £200 / US$375 print or
online
Institutional: £230 / US$431 combined
print and online

Subscription Offices UK
John Wiley & Sons Ltd
Journals Administration Department
1 Oldlands Way, Bognor Regis
West Sussex, PO22 9SA
T: +44 (0)1243 843 272
F: +44 (0)1243 843 232
E: cs-journals@wiley.co.uk

Print ISSN: 0003-8504;
Online ISSN: 1554-2769

Prices are for six issues and include
postage and handling charges.
Individual rate subscriptions must be
paid by personal cheque or credit card.
Individual rate subscriptions may not
be resold or used as library copies.

All prices are subject to change
without notice.

Rights and Permissions
Requests to the Publisher should be
addressed to:
Permissions Department
John Wiley & Sons Ltd
The Atrium
Southern Gate
Chichester
West Sussex PO19 8SQ
England

F: +44 (0)1243 770 620
E: permreq@wiley.co.uk

Front cover: Institute for Computational Design (Achim
Menges) and Institute of Building Structures and Structural
Design (Jan Knippers), ICD/ITKE Research Pavilion 2010,
University of Stuttgart, 2010. © Roland Halbe
Inside front cover: (*Detail*) Institute for Computational
Design (Achim Menges) and Institute of Building
Structures and Structural Design (Jan Knippers), ICD/ITKE
Research Pavilion 2011, University of Stuttgart, 2011.
© ICD/ITKE University of Stuttgart

EDITORIAL
Helen Castle

Since the earliest years of Modernism, machine-aided fabrication has represented the Holy Grail of architecture: a means of exerting greater design control over the construction process and reducing the costs and obstacles that are part and parcel of the conventional building process. By the late 1990s, the onset of CAD-CAM and CNC milling, personified by the high-profile employment of CATIA at the Guggenheim Museum Bilbao (1997) by Frank Gehry, fuelled a whole new pipeline of architectural visions; in his Embryological House Project (2000), for instance, Greg Lynn charismatically conjured up a future in which series of branded homes could be designed and customised like trainers. Though this fantasy is yet to be realised with quite this ease of delivery, architecture schools worldwide have taken up the gauntlet, competing on the size of their laser-cutting and milling machines – with robots now frequently making a guest appearance.

This title of Δ shifts the entire focus for thinking about the production of architecture as one that is entirely technologically focused. Though new technologies such as the employment of industrial robots in the place of computer numerically controlled (CNC) machines open up the possibilities for architectural exploration per se (see Achim Menges and Tobias Schwinn on 'Manufacturing Reciprocities', pp 118–25), they do not alone in themselves provide the *raison d'être* or drive for the ideas and research propagated in *Material Computation*. For Menges, the greatest potential lies in computation's power to provide a better understanding of material behaviour and characteristics and then, in turn, to inform the organisation of matter and form in design. For him, 'compute' is very much a verb rather than a noun, referring to the processing of information, which is as applicable to natural as it is to artificial systems. His Δ Reader, *Computational Design Thinking* (John Wiley & Sons, 2011), edited with Sean Ahlquist, establishes a foundation for such thought in architecture. It looks far beyond the conventional domain of computer-aided architecture, drawing on relevant principles from mathematics and computer science, developmental and evolutionary biology, system science and philosophy.

In this respect, Menges' interest in material computation should be viewed as part of a much bigger research project that he is now pursuing as a professor and director at the Institute for Computational Design (ICD) at the University of Stuttgart, and previously as a studio master of the Emergent Technologies and Design (EmTech) graduate programme at the Architectural Association (AA) in London (see 'About the Guest-Editor', p 7). For Δ, it also represents the fourth in a lineage of highly successful publications on different aspects of morphogenetic design by Menges and his EmTech collaborators at the AA, Michael Hensel and Michael Weinstock. These include: *Emergence: Morphogenetic Design Strategies* (Vol 74, No 3, May/June 2004), *Techniques and Technologies in Morphogenetic Design* (Vol 76, No 2, March/April 2006) and *Versatility and Vicissitude: Performance in Morpho-Ecological Design* (Vol 78, No 2, March/April 2008). Δ

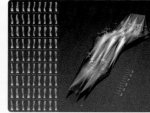
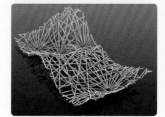

Achim Menges, Steffen Reichert and Scheffler+Partner, FAZ Pavilion, Frankfurt, 2010
top: The pavilion design is derived from biomimetic research investigating autonomous, passively actuated surface structures responsive to changes in ambient humidity based on the biological principles of conifer cones. When the weather changes, the pavilion's envelope adapts to the related increase in relative ambient humidity by closing its weatherproof skin.

Achim Menges with Steffen Reichert, HygroScope – Meteorosensitive Morphology, Centre Pompidou, Paris, 2012
centre: The project explores a novel mode of responsive architecture based on the combination of material inherent behaviour and computational morphogenesis. The dimensional instability of wood in relation to moisture content is employed to construct a highly differentiated architectural envelope that opens and closes in response to climate changes with no need for any technical equipment.

Achim Menges, Morphogenetic Design Experiments 01–05, London, 2002–06
bottom: A series of morphogenetic design experiments investigated the possible integration of physical and computational morphogenetic processes in architecture.

Achim Menges ... derives all his experiments from the concrete world of materials loaded with forces and uses the software environment to capture the geometries that the real world produces and to subject them to systematics. ... He naturally speaks about a 'physiology' of forms in the same way as a biologist: because he has a purchase on actual behaviours – and not only fantasies of behaviours – he can operate on matter in a way not dissimilar to the meshworks of nature. His forms are resultants, not of crude literalisms like 'indexes' but of 'logics' and algorithmic machines. ... Because he has understood that form is an exfoliation of logic – not force – he may be alone to have any claim to being a materialist in the end.
— Sanford Kwinter[1]

Achim Menges' fascination with nature's intricate processes of material articulation and ecological embedding has driven both his architectural practice and his academic work as professor at the University of Stuttgart, and visiting professor at the Harvard University Graduate School of Design (GSD) and the Architectural Association (AA) in London. His multifaceted body of morphogenetic design research investigates a wide range of disciplinary concerns, one of which will be presented in this issue: the possible integration of design computation and materialisation in architecture.

Menges received a diploma with honours from the AA, where he taught as studio master of the Emergent Technologies and Design (EmTech) graduate programme from 2002 to 2009, and as a diploma unit master from 2003 to 2006. Only six years after graduating, he was appointed as tenure professor and director of the Institute for Computational Design (ICD) at the University of Stuttgart, a school renowned for creatively engaging the rigour and insights of engineering science in architectural design, best exemplified by one of its most prolific former institute leaders: Frei Otto. Similar to Otto, Menges conceives of physical and material computation as a potent driver for integrative architectural design. His institute thus investigates ways of synthesising physical and computational morphogenetic processes. It pursues both basic research in design computation and digital fabrication, as well as applied multidisciplinary computational design research with leading industrial partners including Mercedes-Benz's Advanced Design department. In addition to the research and doctorate programmes, the ICD is currently preparing for its first intake of masters students in autumn 2012.

Menges' design work has won numerous international awards, has been exhibited worldwide, and forms part of the permanent collection of, among others, the Centre Pompidou in Paris. He is the editor/author of numerous architectural books and magazines, and has published extensively in internationally renowned architectural magazines and journals. ∆

Note
1. Sanford Kwinter, 'A Conversation Between Sanford Kwinter and Jason Payne', in T Sakamoto, A Ferre and M Kubo (eds), *From Control to Design: Parametric/Algorithmic Architecture*, Actar (Barcelona), 2008, S 226.

Rather than taking raw materials, sending them through a machine or process that is inherently fighting tolerances, errors and energy consumption to arrive at a desired product, we should be directly embedding assembly information into raw materials, then watching as the materials assemble themselves …
— *Skylar Tibbits*

Skylar Tibbits

Logic Matter, Massachusetts Institute of Technology (MIT), Cambridge, Massachusetts, 2010
Logic Matter is a system built upon redundant information. The white units are redundant information used as input for the growth of a structure. They provide structural redundancy and store assembly information like a hard drive. The grey units are the primary unit providing computation and the linear sequence of growth.

ICD + ITKE University
of Stuttgart

ICD/ITKE Research Pavilion 2010,
University of Stuttgart, Stuttgart, 2010
The combination of the pre-stress resulting
from the elastic bending during the
assembly process and the morphological
differentiation of the joint locations enables
a very lightweight and materially efficient
system. The entire pavilion was constructed
using only 6.5-millimetre (¼-inch) thin
birch plywood sheets.

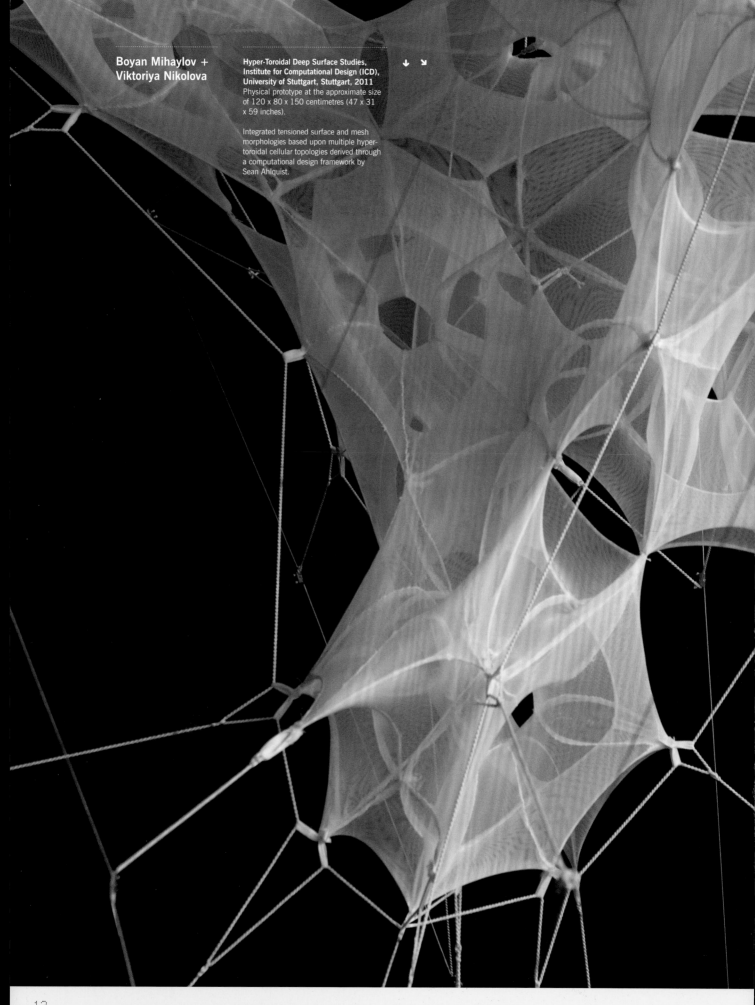

Boyan Mihaylov +
Viktoriya Nikolova

Hyper-Toroidal Deep Surface Studies,
Institute for Computational Design (ICD),
University of Stuttgart, Stuttgart, 2011
Physical prototype at the approximate size
of 120 x 80 x 150 centimetres (47 x 31
x 59 inches).

Integrated tensioned surface and mesh
morphologies based upon multiple hyper-
toroidal cellular topologies derived through
a computational design framework by
Sean Ahlquist.

MATERIAL
COMPUTAT

ION HIGHER INTEGRATION IN MORPHOGENETIC DESIGN

No computer on earth can match the processing power of even the most simple natural system, be it of water molecules on a warm rock, a rudimentary enzyme system, or the movement of leaves in the wind. The most powerful and challenging use of the computer … is in learning how to make a simple organization (the computer) model what is intrinsic about a more complex, infinitely entailed organization (the natural or real system).
— Sanford Kwinter [1]

The production of architecture, both intellectually and physically, is on the brink of a significant change. Computational design enables architects to integrate ever more multifaceted and complex design information, while the industrial logics of conventional building construction are eroding rapidly in a context of increasingly ubiquitous computer-controlled manufacturing and fabrication. A novel convergence of computation and materialisation is about to arise, bringing the virtual processes of computational design and the physical realisation of architecture much closer together, more so than ever before.

Computation, in its basic meaning, refers to the processing of information. Material has the capacity to compute. Long before the much discussed appearance of truly biotic architecture will actually be realised, the conjoining of machine and material computation potentially has significant and unprecedented consequences for design and the future of our built environment. In architecture, computation provides a powerful agency for both informing the design process through specific material behaviour and characteristics, and in turn informing the organisation of matter and material across multiple scales based on feedback with the environment. Circumnavigating the essentialist, idealist and positivist traps that litter the notion of material in architectural history, materiality and materialisation can become the starting points of an exploratory, open-ended design process, and thus serve, quite literally, as the raw materials for design research and architectural inquiry. Material properties, characteristics and behaviour can now be employed as active design generators, and the microscale of material make-up and the macroscale of material systems in architecture can now be understood as a continuum of reciprocal behavioural characteristics and performative capacities.

Formation and Materialisation in Nature

If nature is at all economical (and there is good reason that is often the case, though not invariably so), we can expect that she will choose to create at least some complex forms not by laborious piece-by-piece construction but by harnessing some of the organisational and pattern-forming phenomena we see in the non-living world. Evolution, via genetics, can exploit, tame and tune such phenomena; but it does not necessarily generate them. If this is so, we can expect to see similarities in the forms and patterns of living and purely inorganic systems, and to be able to explain them both in the same manner.
— Philip Ball [2]

Physical computation is at the very core of the emergence of natural systems and forms. While this realisation may initially seem obvious for non-living nature, the critical importance of physical processes for the evolutionary development of living nature has not always been fully recognised. For a long time evolutionary biology was considered to suggest that nature has at its disposal an infinite palette of possibilities, and that the

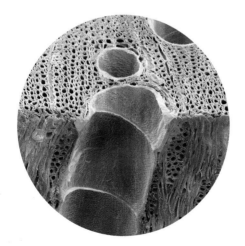

Jian Huang and Minhwan Park, Differentiated Wood Lattice Shell, Performative Wood Studio (Achim Menges), Harvard University Graduate School of Design (GSD), Cambridge, Massachusetts, 2009
previous spread: A computational design tool was developed based on synchronous physical and computational studies and the related encoding of material characteristics and system behaviour, enabling the construction of a differentiated wood lattice shell with a stressed actuator skin.

Coloured scanning electron micrograph (SEM) of a block of wood from an elm tree (*Ulmus procera*)
above: Top: transverse section. Bottom: longitudinal section. Xylem vessels (larger tubes) are seen in the wood. The xylem transports water and mineral nutrients from the roots throughout the plant. Its thick lignin walls also provide structural support for the stem.

evolutionary development of genetic code would be the critical determinant for what natural systems are actualised and how they form. However, with the recent rapid advancement of research in genetics, it seems that the more we know about the genetic code the better we understand the importance of physical processes of material self-organisation and structuring in morphogenesis. In his seminal book series *Nature's Patterns: A Tapestry in Three Parts* (2009), Philip Ball aptly states that 'evolution operates within physical constraints which insist that not everything really is possible'.[3] In his contribution to this issue (pp 22–7), Ball introduces a range of pattern formations in both living and non-living nature, and explains how they can be surprisingly similar because they are driven by analogical processes of simple, local material interactions, which he describes as a form of physical computation that gives rise to material self-organisation and emergent structures and behaviours.

Another critical facet of morphogenesis in nature has been outlined by J Scott Turner in his two seminal books *The Extended Organism* (2000) and *The Tinkerer's Accomplice* (2007).[4] In addition to self-organisation processes driven by physical laws and the stochastic search of evolutionary development, Turner identifies physiological drivers as another critical constituent for the material formation of living systems. In his article for this issue (pp 28–33), he explains how living systems seem to converge on effective 'design' much faster and more predictably than a simple regime of evolutionary selection alone, the Darwin machine, would seem to allow. He argues that what is missing from our conceptions of how design arises in nature is found in another machine metaphor, what we might call the Bernard machine, agents of the little-appreciated concept of homeostasis, the brainchild of Darwin's French contemporary, Claude Bernard. Introducing research on the physiologically driven, continuous material restructuring of bone, Turner's article contributes a critical perspective on how material formation in nature is directly linked to physiological processes and energy systems.

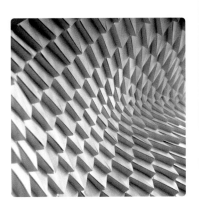

Steffen Reichert, Responsive Surface Structure I, Department for Form Generation and Materialisation, HFG Offenbach, Offenbach am Main, Germany, 2007
A full-scale, functional responsive surface prototype shows how the material's responsive capacity can be explored through a field of surprisingly simple components that are all at the same time embedded sensor, no-energy motor and regulating element.

Design Computation and Materialisation

In contrast to the integral processes of material formation in nature, architecture as a material practice is still predominantly based on design approaches that struggle to fully explore the materials' richness of performative capacity and resourcefulness for design. Because of the primacy of scalar descriptions of geometry emblematic for most contemporary design tools, in the decisive early design stages materiality is usually conceptualised as a mere passive property assigned to geometrically defined elements, and materialisation is implicitly conceived as a secondary process of facilitating a scheme's realisation within the physical world. Consequently, material information is understood as facilitative rather than generative. For almost a decade, I have researched an alternative design approach that unfolds specific material gestalt and related performative capacities by reconciling computational form generation and physical materialisation. In 'Material Resourcefulness: Activating Material Information in Computational Design' (pp 34–43), I outline ways of integrating material information as a generative driver in design computation. Taking wood as an example, the article shows how integrative design computation allows exploration of one of the oldest and most common construction materials as a natural high-performance fibre composite. This opens up the possibility of employing wood's capacity to materially compute both form and responsive performance, which is further elaborated in the following two articles.

Along the example of the interdisciplinary ICD/ITKE Research Pavilion, a novel bending-active structure of extremely thin, elastically bent wood lamellas at the University of Stuttgart, Moritz Fleischmann, Jan Knippers, Julian Lienhard, Simon Schleicher and myself (pp 44–51) explain how feedback between computational design, advanced simulation and robotic fabrication expands the design space towards hitherto unsought architectural possibilities, enabling material behaviour to unfold a complex performative structure from a surprisingly simple material system. In addition to these structural opportunities, the characteristics of wood offer yet another striking design possibility. The hygroscopic behaviour of wood can be exploited in the development of no-tech responsive architecture. In contrast to most contemporary attempts of climate-responsive architecture that heavily rely on elaborate high-tech equipment superimposed on otherwise inert material constructs, here all the responsive capacity is embedded in the structure of the material itself.

Based on the development of wood-composite elements, myself and Steffen Reichert present research on biomimetic responsive material systems that neither require the supply of external energy nor any kind of mechanical or electronic control (pp 52–9). The article introduces ways of physically programming the humidity-reactive behaviour of these material systems, and explains the possibilities this opens up for a strikingly simple yet truly ecologically embedded architecture in constant feedback and interaction with its surrounding environment. The work of Ferdinand Ludwig, Hannes Schwertfeger and Oliver Storz pushes the research on wood even further by investigating how it can be employed as a living construction material (pp 82–7). By designing the growth and physical constitution of trees to develop particular structural and morphological features, their interdisciplinary research with

Institute for Computational Design (Achim Menges) and Institute of Building Structures and Structural Design (Jan Knippers), ICD/ITKE Research Pavilion 2011, University of Stuttgart, Stuttgart, 2011
The development of a generative computational process based on the morphological principles of the plate skeleton of echinoids enabled the design and robotic manufacturing of a modular system that only uses extremely thin (6.5-millimetre/¼-inch) plywood sheets. The pavilion is thus both economical to build and materially highly efficient, while at the same time providing an enriched spatial extension of the university's central public square.

We are beginning to recover a certain philosophical respect for the inherent morphogenetic potential of all materials. And we may now be in a position to think about the origin of form and structure, not as something imposed from the outside on an inert matter, not as a hierarchical command from above as in an assembly line, but as something that may come from within the materials, a form that we tease out of those materials as we allow them to have their say in the structures we create.
— Manuel DeLanda[5]

architects, engineers and biologists synthesises architectural qualities, constructive requirements and biological properties in vegetal-technical compound structures, which provides a surprising facet of forecasting the latent convergence of living and non-living systems in architecture.

In material-based design approaches, computation allows for higher integration on a multitude of levels, ranging from the composition of the material itself to the assembly of systems from multiple material elements to the behaviour of systems of manifold material constituents affecting each other and interacting within a field of various external influences. The following articles provide insights into these different facets of computational design research, thus offering an outlook on how an overall integrative design approach can be conceived. Force-driven material systems, as, for example, pre-tensioned membrane structures, require physics-based design approaches, especially if they consist of multiple levels of hierarchy and many different tensile elements, as they do not follow predictable geometric or mathematical patterns. Here, the material system morphology as an expression of internal and external forces in equilibrium is a subsequence of variable material properties and force distribution characteristics. Sean Ahlquist and myself present research into tension-driven material systems (pp 60–7), and explain the development of an architectural design framework that allows for these complex material interdependencies to be not only resolved, but explored as multiple possible equilibrium states. As a computational process that moves between virtual generation and physical materialisation, the process structure is capable of evolving morphologically complex yet viable tension-active formations.

Both Skylar Tibbits', as well as the article by Karola Dierichs and myself, investigate the formation of larger systems from numerous material elements. Identifying a fundamental lack of finesse in contemporary modes of construction when compared to the increasing sophistication of combined design computation and digital fabrication, Tibbits suggests how today's processes of assembly could be profoundly reimagined (pp 60–73). Looking at biological systems that are building structures with far more complexity, information capacity and assembly instructions than even the most advanced structures possible with our current technologies, he identifies self-assembly as the key ingredient embedded within these natural systems, and outlines an approach for designing systems that build themselves.

Karola Dierichs and myself offer a profoundly different perspective for rethinking construction, by abandoning the notion of assembly altogether and replacing it with aggregation (pp 74–81). Whereas assembly seeks control on the level of connections between fixed elements, aggregation focuses on the overall system behaviour resulting from the interaction of loose elements. Composed of large numbers of unbound yet designed granules, an aggregate architecture is based on a fundamentally different logic of construction: in contrast to assembly systems, aggregates materially compute their overall constructional configuration and shape as spatiotemporal behavioural patterns, with an equal ability for both: the stable character of a solid material and the rapid reconfigurability of a fluid.

Computational Practice and Designed Materiality

The logics of generative computational systems that integrate material, form and performance in the design process offer ways of processing the flow of structural forces and interaction with environmental influences on a material construct and balancing morphological differentiation with the characteristics and behaviour of material. Toni Kotnik and Michael Weinstock (pp 104–11) present a series of experimental construction projects whose emergent material forms have the capacity to respond effectively to forces that will be imposed upon them in the physical world.

In addition to the intricate relations between material, form and performance, computation offers the possibility of integrating processes of manufacturing and fabrication in the design exploration. This is of particular relevance in the context of today's shift from task-specific computer numerically controlled (CNC) machines to more generic industrial robots in the building sector. This change from machine hardware and control software developed to facilitate a specific fabrication process, towards more open-ended and generic fabrication devices, enables architects to design custom fabrication processes and machine-control protocols. The article by myself and Tobias Schwinn (pp 118–26) presents how these advanced machine capabilities expand the interface between design computation and physical materialisation. Based on computational explorations of the reciprocal effects between form, fabrication and performance, the machinic morphospace can be explored in relation to biomimetic design principles, enabling the development of material systems that gain performative capacity through the morphological differentiation of robotically prefabricated building elements.

Integrative design computation is not solely the domain of academic research, but is also explored in cutting-edge architectural and engineering practices. Al Fisher (pp 112–18)

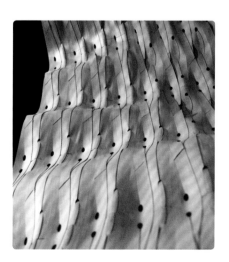

Etien Santiago, Intersective Laminates, Performative Wood Studio (Achim Menges), Harvard University Graduate School of Design (GSD), Cambridge, Massachusetts, 2009
Based on integrative computational design processes, the anisotropic material behaviour of wood is employed in the construction of a morphologically adaptive veneer surface structure.

Institute for Computational Design (Achim Menges) and Institute of Building Structures and Structural Design (Jan Knippers), ICD/ITKE Research Pavilion 2010, University of Stuttgart, Stuttgart, 2010
The innovative structure of the pavilion is entirely based on the elastic bending behaviour of birch plywood strips. The strips are robotically manufactured as planar elements, and subsequently connected, so that elastically bent and tensioned regions alternate along their length. The force that is locally stored in each bent region of the strip, and maintained by the corresponding tensioned region of the neighbouring strip, greatly increases the structural capacity of the system.

Implicit here is the idea of learning how ... to study natural or 'wild' intelligence in a contained but active, refining domain. In this use the computer becomes metallurgical substance, it extends the exploratory evolutionary process of differentiation and refinement by inventing new levels of order and shape.
— Sanford Kwinter[6]

explains the work of Buro Happold's SMART Group on developing real-time simulations where the calculations are persistent within design models that update live as parameters and constraints are manipulated. He shows how lightweight, mobile tools traditionally reserved for detailed design can form the early conceptual stages of design. Interactive models can be tweaked and manipulated, providing a link to the materiality of the design. Through such responsive optimisation environments, hybrid design can be achieved, blending performance with design intent in complex construction projects. Using selected recent projects, Cristiano Ceccato (pp 96–105) explains the work of Zaha Hadid Architects on reconciling advanced forms of digital design that exist within a multidimensional envelope of material performance, production capabilities, logistics and cost, with today's comparatively archaic methods of procurement, fabrication and construction. He illustrates a developing framework of digital architectural practice that is attempting to close the gaps between computational design, digitally controlled manufacturing and evolving mechanisms of contemporary construction.

In the not too distant future, architects will not only be able to employ design computation to integrate and modulate the behaviour and performative capacities of existing materials, but also to design the materiality itself. Inspired by nature's strategies where form-generation is driven by maximal performance with minimal resources through local material property variation, in her article (pp 88–95), Neri Oxman investigates a theoretical and technical framework by which to model, analyse and fabricate objects with non-binary, continuously heterogeneous properties designed to correspond to multiple and continuously varied functional constraints.

One key technology that enables an integrative conception and production of material and structure is rapid prototyping and manufacturing. David Andreen and Rupert Soar (pp 126–35) introduce the different construction-scale additive manufacturing systems currently in development and describe how these technologies provide novel possibilities for addressing architecture's manufacturing challenges in the face of energy expenditure, material resources and environmental impact if linked to physiomimetic computational design strategies.

The issue concludes at this point with Bob Sheil's 'Counterpoint', but scientists are already beginning to investigate the next facet of advancing the research on material computation introduced here by exploring the continuous, exceptionally robust and massively parallel power of *computation in materio*, exploiting the very physics of materials for computational processes. ᗄ

Notes
1. Sanford Kwinter, 'The Computational Fallacy', in Achim Menges and Sean Ahlquist, *Computational Design Thinking*, John Wiley & Sons (London), 2011, p 211.
2. Philip Ball, *Nature's Patterns – Shapes*, Oxford University Press (Oxford), 2009, p 17.
3. Ibid, p 12.
4. J Scott Turner, *The Extended Organism" The Physiology of Animal-Built Structures*, Harvard University Press (Cambridge, MA), 2000. See also: J Scott Turner, *The Tinkerer's Accomplice: How Design Emerges from Life Itself*, Harvard University Press (Cambridge, MA), 2007.
5. Manuel DeLanda, 'Material Complexity', in Neil Leach, David Turnbull and Chris Williams (eds), *Digital Tectonics*, John Wiley & Sons (Chichester), 2004, p 21.
6. Kwinter, op cit, p 213.

Philip Ball

PATTERN FORMATION IN NATURE:
PHYSICAL CONSTRAINTS AND SELF-ORGANISING CHARACTERISTICS

Pattern formations are apparent in natural systems ranging from clouds to animal markings, and from sand dunes to shells of microscopic marine organisms. Despite the astonishing range and variety of such structures, many have comparable features. In this article, **Philip Ball** reviews some of the common patterns found in nature. He explains how they are typically formed through simple, local interactions between many components of a system – a form of physical computation that gives rise to self-organisation and emergent structures and behaviours.

The Giant's Causeway in County Antrim, Ireland.

When the naturalist Joseph Banks first encountered Fingal's Cave on the Scottish island of Staffa, he was astonished by the quasi-geometric, prismatic pillars of rock that flank the entrance. As Banks put it:

> Compared to this what are the cathedrals or palaces built by men! Mere models or playthings, as diminutive as his works will always be when compared with those of nature. What now is the boast of the architect! *Regularity*, the only part in which he fancied himself to exceed his mistress, Nature, is here found in her possession, and here it has been for ages undescribed.[1]

This structure has a counterpart on the coast of Ireland: the Giant's Causeway in County Antrim, where again one can see the extraordinarily regular and geometric honeycomb structure of the fractured igneous rock.

When we make an architectural pattern like this, it is through careful planning and construction, with each individual element cut to shape and laid in place. Our experience from human technologies thus suggests that making a pattern requires a patterner. But at Fingal's Cave and the Giant's Causeway, the forces of nature have conspired to produce a pattern without, we must presume, any blueprint or foresight or design. This is an example of spontaneous pattern formation.[2]

In earlier times, such regularity in nature was taken as evidence of God's guiding hand. We now know that no intelligent agency is needed to create the patterns that appear profusely in both the living and the inorganic natural world. These organised arrays of elements arise spontaneously from the interactions between their many component parts, whether these are chemical reagents that react and diffuse, small particles or molecules that cohere into clusters, propagating cracks, wind-blown sand grains or flowing liquids. Such patterns are said to be self-organised. Their scientific study comprises one aspect of research into so-called complex systems, which typically show emergent behaviours that cannot be deduced or predicted by a focus on the properties of the individual elements.

Such regularities are not just a feature of the insensate or instinctive natural world, but may also be found in human social systems that are seemingly subject to the whims of free will; for example, in the evenly spaced waves of congestion that might appear in moving traffic, or quasi-periodic cycles in economic systems. Understanding how spontaneous pattern formation occurs is therefore an endeavour that unites many disparate fields of science, from zoology to fracture mechanics, and from chemical kinetics to sociology. Many patterns in nature have a universal aspect that does not respect the traditional divisions between the natural sciences, or even between the living and the non-living world. Rather, natural patterns seem to come from a relatively limited palette, even in systems that might seem to have nothing at all in common with one another. The hexagonal columns of Fingal's Cave may put us in mind of other natural hexagonal forms. Do these patterns really have anything in common, or is the similarity in appearance just coincidence?

The first person to confront this question in a systematic way was the Scottish zoologist D'Arcy Wentworth Thompson in his book *On Growth and Form* (1917),[3] which collected together all that was then known about

pattern and form in nature in a synthesis of biology, natural history, mathematics, physics and engineering. Thompson pointed out that, in biology at least, and often in the non-living world, pattern formation is not a static thing, but arises from growth: everything is what it is because it got that way.

The answer to the riddle of pattern lies in how it got to be that way. This is less obvious than it sounds: a bridge or a paddy field or a microchip is 'explained' by how it looks, not how it was made. Thompson objected to the fact that Darwinian, adaptive explanations of form and pattern in living systems tended to take that approach too. The zebra's stripes might be explained in one sense by invoking the adaptive benefit of their camouflage (although in fact the effectiveness of the stripes for concealment is still debated), but this does not account for how any particular zebra acquires these pigmented markings on its hide as it grows from an embryo. Thompson argued that evolutionary biology needs to take into account both the limitations imposed and the possibilities provided by purely physical forces (including chemical processes) acting on a growing organism.

It is now understood that the common features of many natural patterns result from mathematical analogies and equivalences

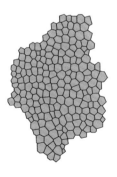

Understanding how spontaneous pattern formation occurs is therefore an endeavour that unites many disparate fields of science, from zoology to fracture mechanics, and from chemical kinetics to sociology.

left: Close-up of the prismatic cross sections of rock columns in the Giant's Causeway.
right: The crack network of a representative section, showing the quasi-hexagonal pattern.

23

in the rules governing their formation – whether these rules are expressed in terms of continuum equations describing, say, diffusion and transport of material, or as local interactions between the components. Both descriptions tend to give rise to solutions that involve symmetry-breaking of an initially uniform or random system, creating spatial and/or temporal segregation of the constituents. These solutions are often modified by specific circumstances such as boundary conditions, the appearance of defects, and path-dependent hysteresis in transitions between patterns. At root, however, they expose self-organisation as an inherent property of complex systems.

Chemical Patterns

An explanation for the patterning apparent in animal markings – noted, but barely explored, by D'Arcy Thompson – has emerged from the study of so-called oscillating chemical reactions, in which a mixture of chemical reagents seems first to react in one direction and then to reverse and reform the original mixture.[4] The classic example is the Belousov-Zhabotinsky (BZ) reaction discovered in the 1960s, in which the mixture alternates between red and blue owing to changes in the charge state of the iron ions that catalyse the reactions. If these oscillations went on indefinitely, the system would violate the second law of thermodynamics. But eventually they die out and the mixture settles into an equilibrium state. Thermodynamics is silent

about the progress of a chemical reaction, but pronounces only on its final, stable state. The oscillations occur only so long as the system is out of equilibrium. It can be maintained in that state indefinitely, however, by continually feeding in fresh reagents and carrying away the end products.

If the mixture is stirred, the colour change takes place more or less everywhere at once. But if the reaction proceeds in an undisturbed thin layer of liquid – or better still, a gel, to slow diffusion and suppress fluid-dynamic disturbances – parts of it can undergo the switch at different times. This does not just produce a patchwork, but regular patterns of concentric bands and spirals: chemical waves that spread through the medium, like the expanding ripples of a stone thrown into a pond. Where two wave fronts meet, they annihilate each other.

The oscillations arise because the reaction has two possible states or branches. Each branch involves an autocatalytic process: the reaction products promote the formation of more of themselves. This is a positive feedback process, and it means that each branch eventually exhausts itself as the feedback speeds up the reaction and depletes the ingredients. When that happens, the system becomes primed to switch to the other branch. The oscillating process depends on two general factors: the ingredients are reacting to produce the coloured products, and the molecules involved are moving by diffusion through the liquid. How quickly the system switches between the red and blue states then depends on how quickly diffusion brings in fresh ingredients to replenish those that have been lost by reaction. So the patterns here come from a balance between reaction, which destroys the ingredients, and diffusion, which replenishes them. This kind of process is known as a reaction-diffusion system. Notice that the pattern comes about through a competition between these two opposing processes. This is one of the universal principles of pattern formation: it requires a balance of opposite tendencies.

In 1952 Alan Turing identified another kind of chemical reaction-diffusion process, which produces not moving chemical waves but stationary patterns.[5] Turing's theory was prompted by the question of how pattern formation occurs in the earliest stages of embryo formation on a fertilised egg. This is a problem of symmetry-breaking: a spherically symmetrical ball of identical cells becomes differentiated into those that will form the head, the limbs, the spine and so forth.

top: A quasi-hexagonal pattern is evident in the markings on a giraffe.

centre: A hexagonal mesh in the shells of microscopic sea creatures (radiolarians).

bottom: Snapshot of chemical-wave patterns in the oscillating Belousov-Zhabotinsky reaction.

Turing suggested that the patterns could be created by two types of chemical substance (morphogens' or 'shape-formers'), both of them diffusing through the system. One is called an activator, because it catalyses its own formation: it is again autocatalytic. The other morphogen is a substance that interferes with this self-generation by the activator: it is, in other words, an inhibitor.[6] Turing showed that stationary patterns – persistent differences in the concentrations of the activator and inhibitor from one part of the system to another – can arise if the inhibitor diffuses more quickly than the activator.

Turing's model generates two particular kinds of pattern: spots and stripes. These predictions were verified when Turing patterns were first produced experimentally in the 1990s.[7] The theory suggests a mechanism for animal markings: during embryo growth, diffusing morphogens imprint the skin with patterns that either switch on pigment-generating genes or leave them off.[8] Turing-type models can explain many of the features of animal markings, for example on fish,[9] wildcats[10] and ladybirds.[11] Specific morphogens responsible for these patterns have not yet been identified, but they have in the analogous case of the regular positioning of hair follicles in mammals.[12]

Granular Patterns

The stripes of the zebra might put us in mind of the ripple formations in wind-blown sand.[13] It has been argued that the formation of sand ripples and dunes can also be regarded as a process involving localised activation and longer-ranged suppression. The appearance of a ripple is a self-activating or autocatalytic process: as soon as a tiny bump grows on a flat surface that is being scattered with wind-blown sand, it starts to capture more grains than the surrounding surface, and so it grows bigger.[14] And the bigger it gets, the more grains it captures. At the same time, this means that the wind gets depleted of its grains, and so there is less chance of another ripple developing in the lee of an existing one: there is inhibition around the ripple, so that the next ripple has to be a certain minimum distance away.

Dunes are created in a similar process, modified by factors such as wind dynamics, local topography and vegetation. Sand may become self-organised in this way into a variety of structures, including straight and undulating (seif) ripple dunes, crescent-shaped barchan dunes and many-armed star dunes. On the granular surface of Mars,

differences in gravity, atmospheric pressure and wind speed give rise to some quite new types of dune shape not seen on earth.

Systems of interacting grains can form a wide variety of patterns. For example, a very thin layer of spherical metal grains vertically vibrated in a shallow, sealed and evacuated container will form stationary waves called oscillons in which the grains are constantly rising and falling in step with each other.[15] These waves will become self-organised into regular arrays of stripes, spirals, hexagonal and square cells, and more random, non-stationary cell-like patterns that appear to be turbulent. The pattern selected depends on the frequency and amplitude of the shaking, and switches between patterns happen abruptly as critical thresholds are crossed. These patterns result from collisions between grains, which put the grains literally 'in touch' with one another so that their movements may become synchronised. The patterns can be reproduced in a model which assumes merely that the grains lose a little energy when they collide.[16]

If such 'grains' may move of their own accord, and interact via relatively simple rules of attraction, repulsion and mimicry, as some animal populations do, they can display the kinds of coordinated swarming patterns seen

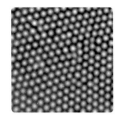

Thermodynamics is silent about the progress of a chemical reaction, but pronounces only on its final, stable state.

top: The generic forms of stationary chemical patterns (Turing patterns): spots and stripes.

centre and bottom: Schemes based on Turing patterns have been proposed to explain the markings on wildcats, fish and ladybirds.

for fish and birds.[17] Simple models based on the emergent behaviour of many interacting particles have also been used to account for branching and aggregation patterns, which may be as regular as those of snowflakes[18] or as apparently disorderly as those of river networks[19] and cities.[20]

Patterns As Computation

There is – despite aspirations to the contrary – no universal theory of pattern formation in nature. Nonetheless, it has proved possible to identify many common principles, such as the universality of certain basic forms (hexagons, stripes, hierarchical branches, fractal shapes, spirals), the importance of non-equilibrium growth processes, the balance or to-and-fro between conflicting driving forces, and the existence of sharp thresholds of driving force that produce global changes in the pattern. The pseudo-hexagonal cracks of Fingal's Cave and the Giant's Causeway seem to emerge as a near-optimal way of releasing the tension that builds up in molten rock as it cools, hardens and contracts: an orderly energetic minimum selected from an initially random arrangement of cracks in an iterative manner as the cracks descend through the solidifying material,[21] balancing forces in a manner – and with a result – not unlike that found in foams.[22]

In general, self-organised patterns can be regarded as a kind of computation performed by the interactions of physical particles. This is made most apparent in models based on cellular automata: discrete elements (cells) organised on a regular grid, which interact via simple, local rules that depend on the state of neighbouring cells. Cellular automata were first invoked by John von Neumann and Stanislas Ulam in the 1950s within the context of a generalised theory of computation: each cell can be considered as a 'memory' cell encoding information in its physical state. Von Neumann was interested in whether such automata might be able to replicate patterns of information and thereby to evolve into more complex computational states, ultimately displaying a form of 'thinking'. The capacity of cellular automata to spawn complex patterns that can replicate or move across the grid was revealed in the Game of Life, a particular cellular automaton devised in the 1960s by the mathematician John Horton Conway. The connections both with computation and with self-organised patterns has been extensively investigated by Wolfram.[23] The patterns that have been described here, including chemical waves,[24] can be reproduced in models based on cellular automata rather than, for example, continuum equations of chemical diffusion and kinetics. This illustrates how spontaneous patterning is a general property of complex systems of many components, interacting via local rules that are often relatively simple.

In the living world, pattern formation seems both to constrain adaptive change and to offer new adaptive opportunities – to operate, in other words, in parallel and sometimes in sympathy with Darwinian evolution. The technological and aesthetic possibilities of spontaneous pattern formation, for example in materials science, architecture and the production of structurally and dynamically complex chemical systems, is only just beginning to be explored. ∆

There is – despite aspirations to the contrary – no universal theory of pattern formation in nature. Nonetheless, it has proved possible to identify many common principles, such as the universality of certain basic forms (hexagons, stripes, hierarchical branches, fractal shapes, spirals)

top: On Mars, differences in wind speed, gravity and atmospheric pressure may create new dunes shapes.

above: Granular materials are prolific pattern-formers. Sand ripples seem to have the same sinuous form as a zebra's stripes. Sand dunes are analogous structures on larger scales.

Notes

1. In O Goldsmith, *A History of the Earth and Animated Earth*, Volume I, Blackie & Son (Glasgow), 1855, p 33.
2. See Philip Ball, *The Self-Made Tapestry*, Oxford University Press (Oxford), 1999, and Philip Ball, *Nature's Patterns*, Oxford University Press (Oxford), 2009.
3. D'Arcy Wentworth Thompson, *On Growth and Form*, Cambridge University Press (Cambridge), 1917.
4. See Arthur Winfree, *When Time Breaks Down*, Princeton University Press (Princeton, NJ), 1987, and Stephen K Scott, *Oscillations, Waves and Chaos in Chemical Kinetics*, Oxford University Press (Oxford), 1994.
5. AM Turing, 'The Chemical Basis of Morphogenesis', *Philosophical Transactions of the Royal Society* B 237, 1952, pp 37–72.
6. A Gierer and H Meinhardt, 'A Theory of Biological Pattern Formation', *Kybernetik* 12, 1972, pp 30–9.
7. See V Castets, E Dulos, J Boissonade and P De Kepper, 'Experimental Evidence of a Sustained Standing Turing-Type Non-Equilibrium Chemical Pattern', *Physical Review Letters* 64, 1990, pp 2953–6, and Q Ouyang and HL Swinney, 'Transition from a Uniform State to Hexagonal and Striped Turing Patterns', *Nature* 352, 1991, pp 610–12.
8. See James D Murray, *Mathematical Biology*, Springer (Berlin), 1990, and Hans Meinhardt, *Models of Biological Pattern Formation*, Academic Press (London), 1982.
9. S Kondo and R Asai, 'A Reaction-Diffusion Wave on the Skin of the Marine Angelfish *Pomacanthus*', *Nature* 376, 1995, pp 765–8.
10. RT Liu, SS Liaw and PK Maini, 'Two-Stage Turing Model for Generating Pigment Patterns on the Leopard and the Jaguar', *Physical Review* E 74, 2006, 011914.
11. SS Liaw, CC Yang, RT Liu & JT Hong, 'Turing Model for the Patterns of Lady Beetles', *Physical Review* E 64, 2001, 041909.
12. S Sick, S Reinker, J Timmer and T Schlake, 'WNT and DKK Determine Hair Follicle Spacing Through a Reaction-Diffusion Mechanism', *Science* 314, 2006, pp 1447–50.
13. Ralph A Bagnold, *The Physics of Wind-Blown Sand and Desert Dunes*, Methuen (London), 1941.
14. SB Forrest and PK Haff, 'Mechanics of Wind Ripple Stratigraphy', *Science* 255, 1992, pp 1240–3.
15. See PM Umbanhowar, F Melo and HL Swinney, 'Localized Excitations in a Vertically Vibrated Granular Layer', *Nature* 382, 1996, pp 793–6, and PM Umbanhowar, F Melo and HL Swinney, 'Periodic, Aperiodic and Transient Patterns in Vibrated Granular Layers'. *Physica* A 249, 1998, pp 1–9.
16. T Shinbrot, 'Competition Between Randomizing Impacts and Inelastic Collisions in Granular Pattern Formation', *Nature* 389, 1997, pp 574–6.
17. See A Czirók and T Vicsek, 'Collective Behavior of Interacting Self-Propelled Particles', *Physica* A 281, 2000, pp 17–29, and ID Couzin and J Krause, 'Self-Organization and Collective Behavior in Vertebrates', *Advances in the Study of Behavior* 32, 2003, pp 1–75.
18. K Libbrecht, 'The Formation of Snow Crystals', *American Scientist* 95 (1), 2007, pp 52–9.
19. Ignacio Rodriguez-Iturbe and Andrea Rinaldo, *Fractal River Basins: Chance and Self-Organization*, Cambridge University Press (Cambridge), 1997.
20. Michael Batty and Paul Longley, *Fractal Cities*, Academic Press (London), 1994.
21. EA Jagla and AG Rojo, 'Sequential Fragmentation: the Origin of Columnar Quasihexagonal Patterns', *Physical Review* E 65, 2002, 026203.
22. Denis Weaire, *The Kelvin Problem*, Taylor & Francis (London), 1996.
23. Stephen Wolfram, *A New Kind of Science*, Wolfram Media Inc (Champaign, IL), 2002.
24. M Markus and B Hess, 'Isotropic Cellular Automaton for Modelling Excitable Media', *Nature* 347, 1990, pp 56–8.

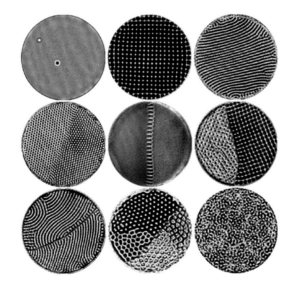

Vertically vibrated grains will self-organise into isolated waves (oscillons) or a variety of patterns including extended standing waves.

EVOLUTI

SOME PERSPECTIVES FROM

ARCHITE

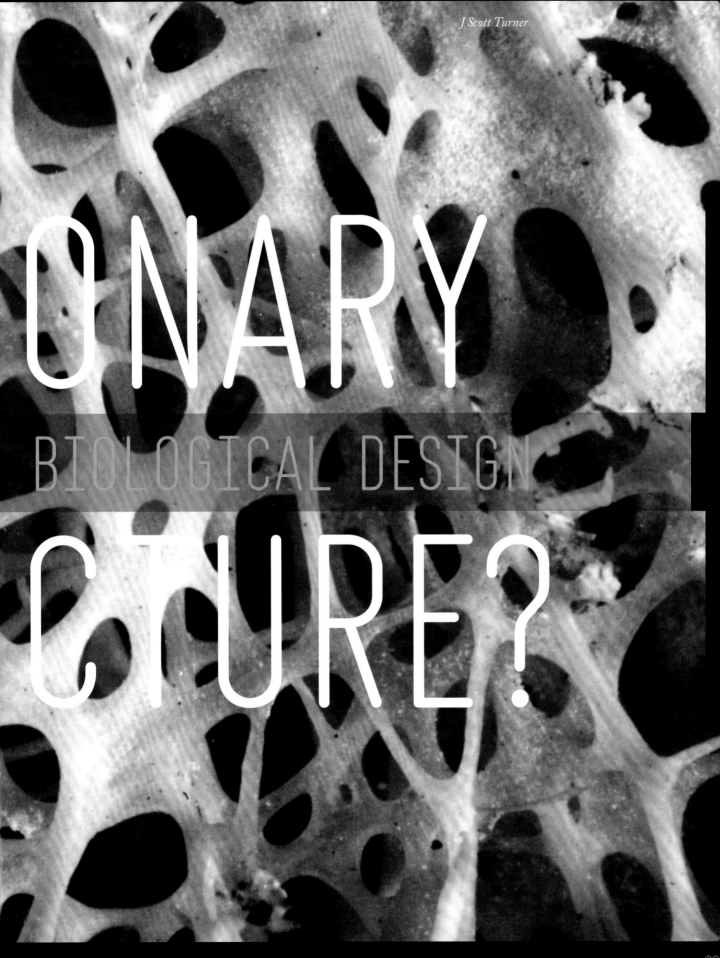

ONARY

BIOLOGICAL DESIGN

CTURE?

J Scott Turner

Architects' view of nature tends to rest on the assumption that it is inherently efficient in its use of materials and energy, and essentially ingenious and elegant in its solutions. This perception in science is one that has been propounded through Darwinism: the notion that refinement of 'design' is achieved through repetitive selection, variation and mutation. The renowned biologist **J Scott Turner** argues here that there is little evidence that living design actually comes about in this way. Instead, looking to Darwin's French contemporary Claude Bernard and his theory of homeostasis, he proposes that living systems converge on effective design much faster and more predictably than a simple regime of natural selection alone would suggest.

Is an architect wise to look to living nature for inspiration? That depends, as often is the case, on what inspiration one draws. Is it nature's elegant beauty that inspires – the delicate meshwork of a feather, the cathedral-like arches of a forest canopy, the stunning colours of a flower? Or is it the marvellous efficiency and versatility that seems to ooze from life, refined by generation upon generation of remorseless natural selection?

It is easy to assume that, because elegant form and efficient function really do go so often together in the living world, that taking care of one will, *mirabile dictu*, take care of the other. That is the faith that underpins biomimetic architecture: look to living nature for an elegant solution to some problem – holding up a roof, ventilating a space, managing a climate, channelling light. Construct something that looks like the original and it will perform like the original. Or plaster life onto your design somehow – living walls, contained swamps, cloud generators – and the services that cost so much to provide when we build machines into a building will emerge, on their own, and nearly for free. Yet, elegant form and efficient function do not always blend so seamlessly in living nature; indeed, it is a good thing that they do not, for natural selection could not work if they did. And it may come as a surprise to learn that we biologists are not entirely sure just how living things themselves manage to pull off the trick.

When biologists encounter living design, we reflexively turn to the power of natural selection to explain it. There is a useful metaphor to explain this process: the Darwin machine. Each generation is a kind of experiment: genetic variation means that each individual represents a slightly different 'hypothesis'

Scanning electron micrograph (SEM) of cancellous (spongy) bone of the human shin
previous spread: Bone tissue is either compact or cancellous. Compact bone usually makes up the exterior of the bone, while cancellous bone is found in the interior. Cancellous bone is characterised by a honeycomb arrangement of trabeculae. These structures help to provide support and strength. The spaces within this tissue normally contain bone marrow, a blood-forming substance.

Coloured scanning electron micrograph (SEM) of osteoblast bone cells on a section of bone
opposite: Osteoblasts are bone cells (osteocytes) in the process of forming new bone tissue. The cells produce osteoid, a matrix of collagen fibres and glycoproteins. Once this is produced by the cell, calcium salts crystallise inside it, making it hard and mineralised.

about how to live in an environment. Some individuals represent good genetic 'guesses', while for others the odds are longer. Those that have the guess right become the fecund ones who make the next generation and run the next experiment, while the losers are shouldered from the table. And so it goes, generation upon generation, try upon try, each crank of the Darwin machine refining the range of guesses until the world is eventually populated by the descendants of consistent winners. From this relentless grinding comes the living world's marvellous diversity and ingenuity that so inspires architects and designers. But in the realm of the Darwin machine, the marvels are illusory: it is Cruel Fortune who rules the game, and the players live or die according to her fickle whim. There is an awful beauty to this.

Before there was Charles Darwin (1809–82), there was an alternative view of evolution, this one promulgated several decades prior by a French biologist, Jean-Baptiste Pierre Antoine de Monet, Chevalier de Lamarck (1744–1829) – his name is thankfully now shortened to his honorific Lamarck. Today, biologists mainly remember Lamarck as a foil to the great Darwin, someone who elevated evolutionism to respectability but otherwise got the explanation completely wrong. The story of the giraffe's long neck is all that is left today of Lamarck's evolutionary thought: giraffes have long necks because generations of their short-necked ancestors stretched their necks to reach high leaves on trees. We celebrate Darwin because he banished such nonsensical just-so stories for ever from respectable science.

Charles Darwin was indeed a man of many virtues, but a peek behind the hagiography reveals that 'scourge of Lamarck' cannot really be counted among them. Darwin was

himself very Lamarckian in his outlook, as for both him and Lamarck it was adaptation – the cumulative striving for a 'good fit' between an organism and its environment – that was the primary driver of evolution. Where Darwin and Lamarck differed was over a larger question of ultimate goals. Lamarck saw a striving for ever-increasing complexity in evolution, culminating in the emergence of man. Darwin rejected this idea, seeing survival in the immediate 'struggle for existence' as the only goal.

This is not simply an arcane point of scientific history. It is from adaptation that the beautiful coherency of form and function emerges that so inspires biologist, engineer and architect. It should therefore be troubling to learn that the Darwin machine, seemingly so sensible an idea, actually offers no understanding for how this coherency comes about. In the Darwin machine, the organism, for all its beautiful complexity, is now merely the vehicle for the presentation of 'apt function' genes to the scrutiny of indifferent nature. This is a perverse inversion of Darwin's own idea, for it elevates heredity, not adaptation, to being the primary driver of evolution. This leads the biologist into a difficult tautology: an apt function gene is selected because it specifies apt function. For the architect, the Darwin machine offers no guarantee that structure and function are necessarily coherent in the living world. Indeed, it guarantees exactly the opposite, for the Darwin machine needs incoherency to operate. How is the architect, then, to distinguish the claptrap or bad design so he can reliably emulate the good ones? The Darwin machine is no help.

The solution may reside in a machine of another kind, this one named after Charles Darwin's contemporary, the great French physiologist Claude Bernard (1813–78). Like

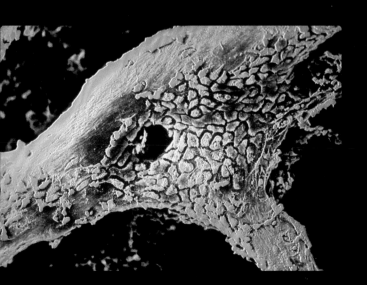

But in the realm of the Darwin machine,
the marvels are illusory: it is Cruel Fortune
who rules the game, and the players live or
die according to her fickle whim.

his countryman Lamarck before him, Bernard was struck by the complexity, coherency and resiliency of living things. Unlike Lamarck, who was a great spinner of grand theoretical systems, Bernard was an experimentalist, teasing out mechanisms – how appetite was regulated, what controlled the flow of blood, what kept the body temperature just so. From his painstaking work came Bernard's signature idea, homeostasis: 'The constancy of the internal environment is the condition for a free and independent life.' Bernard stated it, if anything, too narrowly: homeostasis is a profound, and often misunderstood, assertion about the distinctive nature of life. Although Bernard himself was not an evolutionist, his concept has important evolutionary implications, for it holds within it the key to the core phenomenon of adaptation, and for restoring what the Darwin machine seeks to deprive: the purposeful striving of living systems to survive and prosper. In short, adaptation is the product, not of the soulless grinding of the Darwin machine, but of the hopeful striving of the Bernard machine.

Bones provide a useful example of how a Bernard machine works. There is little question that bones are remarkably well-designed structures. They must support both static and dynamic loads, and they must do so under often-unpredictable conditions. They must serve locomotion, transmitting work efficiently from muscle to the outside world, to propel animals forward, stop them, or turn them on a dime. If an engineer was called upon to design a bone from scratch, he could barely improve upon what nature has already invented. The long bones of the legs or arms, for example, are hollow, like box beams, distributing expensive load-bearing material just to where it is needed. Within, bones bear their loads with elegant

webs of mineralised tissue, reminiscent of the finest Gothic cathedrals. How do bones manage this beautiful design?

It is homeostasis that does it. Bone is a living, dynamic structure, populated by a diverse array of cells that work to continuously remodel it. On the one hand, the osteoclasts are miniature bone bulldozers, ploughing into bones to chip away tiny pieces of calcium phosphate so that these precious materials can be returned to the blood. Within the bone live other cells, the osteocytes, which draw calcium and phosphate from the blood and lay it down like mortar, mineralising and strengthening the bone. The bone's structure is essentially therefore a competition between the osteoclasts tearing it down and osteocytes building it up. If osteoclasts are winning, bone is whittled away and weakens. If osteocytes prevail, the bone builds up and is strengthened. In a mature bone with a stable structure, the two cell types have reached an accommodation: osteocytes laying down new bone just as fast as osteoclasts take it away. This puts good bone design in its proper perspective: it is ensuring that the accommodation between osteocytes and osteoclasts converges at the point where function and structure are optimised.

What ensures that convergence is a Bernard machine at work. Osteocytes do not just lay down mineral; they also monitor the strains that permeate the bone that surrounds them. If the strains are too high, this is an indicator that the surrounding bone is too weak. The osteocytes then ramp up mineralisation, strengthening the bone, and reducing strain until it reaches the point where the osteocytes want it. It works the other way, too. If the osteocytes sense too little strain, this is an indicator that the bone is wastefully over-mineralised. The osteocytes then ease up on mineralisation,

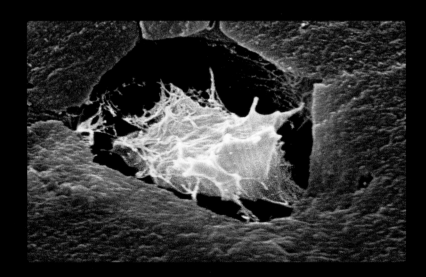

which allows the osteoclasts to temporarily prevail. Bone breaks down and strain increases until they reach the 'sweet spot': just the right amount of strain. As long as the bone is alive, this back-and-forth, building bone up here, breaking it down there, continues until eventually every place in the bone is bearing the same amount of strain. Structure is matched elegantly to function, and everywhere the bone is optimally bearing its load. Thus, it is not genetic specification – a Darwin machine – that is responsible for the bone's good design, but a Bernard machine – the osteocytes' capability for strain homeostasis. In a profound sense, bones are well designed because they want to be well designed. They 'know' when their design falls short, and they take active steps to remedy the shortcomings.

For the biologist committed to the Darwinian idea, the Bernard machine poses a difficult problem, because it seems to reintroduce motivations, desires, even intentionality back where these nebulous ideas had long been thought to be safely banished. The Darwin machine recognises no intention, no desire, no control over destiny. The Bernard machine not only recognises these things, but also asserts that they are the most important things about life. If this is the case, then might evolving lineages control their own evolutionary destiny? That is where the logic of the Bernard machine leads us, but it is not logic alone that seals the deal. Once one knows how to look for Bernard machines, one starts to see them everywhere: in the design of blood vessel networks, of digestive and respiratory systems, even in the origins of cognition and conscious awareness. Never mind the logic of the thing, it is living nature itself that provides the emphatic evidence: the living world is rife with purpose and intentionality, not only in its daily existence, but in its evolution as well. Life is not at the mercy of indifferent nature; life is nature's master.

For the architect, this may be the guide for how to profitably emulate the living world. Architects seek to create environments that are equable to the inhabitants of their creations. There are many ways to do this, but the way living nature does it is through the operational, bottom-up striving for comfort that is implicit in homeostasis. This means that living design is not specified or imposed, but emerges from self-created structures that are dynamically responsive to the inhabitants' comfort: bones are well designed because the osteocytes strive to provide themselves a comfortable environment. Where modern evolution has gone wrong is in assuming that it is the specifiers – genes – that are responsible for good living design. In seeking to emulate living nature in their designs, architects would do well to not repeat our mistake. ⚏

Coloured scanning electron micrograph (SEM) of a freeze-fractured bone cell (osteocyte) surrounded by bone
An osteocyte is called an osteoblast when it is forming bone. It produces osteoid, the organic bone matrix that is a mass of collagen fibres and glycoprotein cement. As soon as osteoid is formed, calcium salts crystallise inside it to form hard, mineralised bone.

There is little question that bones are remarkably well-designed structures. They must support both static and dynamic loads, and they must do so under often-unpredictable conditions. They must serve locomotion, transmitting work efficiently from muscle to the outside world, to propel animals forward, stop them, or turn them on a dime.

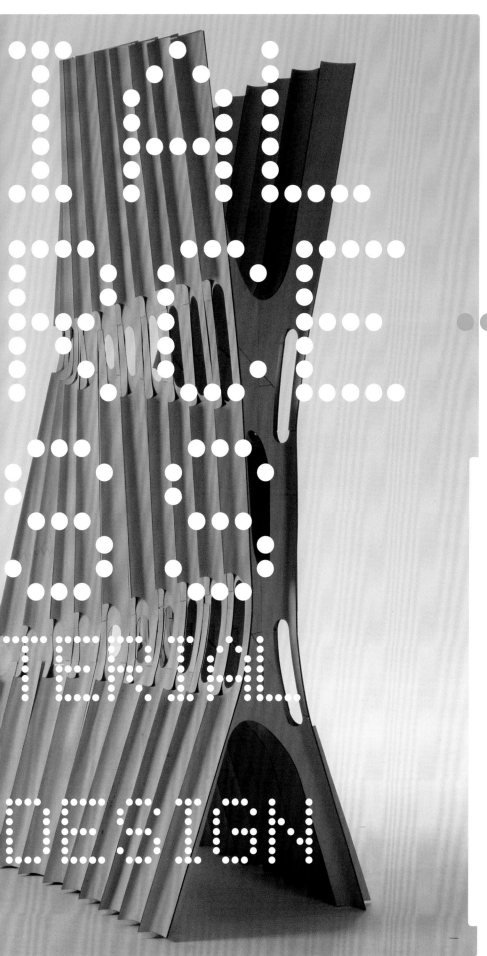

MATERIAL SYSTEMS, COMPUTATIONAL MORPHOGENESIS AND PERFORMATIVE CAPACITY TECHNICAL DESIGN

Recent years have seen the unprecedented innovation of new technologies for the advancement of architectural design. Despite the propensity of complex geometries, elaborate forms and articulated surfaces, information technology has left some profound aspects of design largely unchallenged. A persistently hierarchical approach has often led to the generation of geometric information being prioritised over its subsequent materialisation. Through the example of wood, one of the oldest and most common construction materials, **Achim Menges** here demonstrates how material information should become a generative driver rather than an afterthought in design computation.

Computational design has been employed and explored in
architecture for more than 50 years. From early on, research
into design computation investigated ways of generating,
rather than drawing, design solutions.[1] However, many of
these attempts at employing computers as proper information
processors rather than drawing machines have been
overshadowed by the concurrent development and commercial
success of computer-aided design (CAD) as the predominant
design tool in architectural practice. But CAD is still deeply
rooted in long-established ways of design thinking based on
representational design techniques that promote a hierarchical
relationship between form and material information. It is
innate to the representational nature of CAD that materiality
is conceptualised as a mere passive property assigned to
geometrically defined elements, and that material information
is understood as facilitative rather than generative.[2]

In parallel to the development of CAD, a wide variety
of generative computational design techniques have been
both researched in academia and employed in practice. In
computational design form-generation, information and
performance are more inherently related, but most often
this integrative character is directed towards the inclusion of
programmatic, economic or environmental information as
operative design and feedback criteria. In contrast, material
information is still hardly ever considered, let alone utilised,
as a generative driver. It seems that the omnipresence of
CAD and its inherently shape-oriented representational
design techniques has preconditioned contemporary design
thinking to such a degree that, even in design computation,
materiality is still conceived as a passive property of form
rather than as an active form-generator. But unlike CAD,
the underlying logic of computational design does offer the
possibility of synthesising virtual form generation and physical
materialisation in architectural design.

Material Information

In one philosophy one thinks of form or design as primarily
conceptual or cerebral, something to be generated as a pure
thought in isolation from the messy world of matter and
energy. Once conceived, a design can be given a physical
form by simply imposing it on a material substratum, which
is taken to be homogeneous, obedient and receptive to
the wishes of the designer. ... The opposite stance may be
represented by a philosophy of design in which materials
are not inert receptacles for a cerebral form imposed from
the outside, but active participants in the genesis of form.
This implies the existence of heterogeneous materials, with
variable properties and idiosyncrasies which the designer
must respect and make an integral part of the design which,
it follows, cannot be routinized.
— Manuel DeLanda[3]

This article will present a design approach that allows the
innate characteristics, behaviour and capacities of the material
systems that define the very physicality of architecture to
play a more active role in design computation. Material
information cannot only be integrated in computational design;
it can act as one of its generative morphogenetic drivers. In
this way the properties and behaviour of material and the
related characteristics of materialisation are not understood as
constituting constraints that merely need to be accommodated,
but rather as being the very source of an exploratory
computational design process.[4]

Employing computation to tap into the intricate and
multifaceted design potential latent in the material itself enables
the development of material systems that no longer need to
be derivatives of long-established and standardised building
systems and elements.[5] Conceiving the microscale of the
material make-up, and the macroscale of the material system as
continuums of reciprocal relations opens up a vast search space

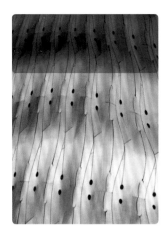

for design, as most materials are complex and display non-linear behaviour when exposed to dynamic environmental influences and forces. Computation allows navigating and discovering unknown points within this search space, and thus enables an exploratory design process of unfolding material-specific gestalt and related performative capacity. Moreover, it allows design to critically question, reassess and free itself from all the idealist and positivist preconceptions the notion of materiality in architecture is still loaded with.

Material-based computational design processes can operate in the context of using existing materials or even designing new materials. While the latter surely is interesting, the former already offers a surprising wealth of novel design opportunities. The focus below will therefore be on the computational design integration of one the oldest and most common construction materials: wood.

Material Integration: Performative Wood

Why should one relate an innovative computational design approach to what initially appears as a fairly archaic building material? In the light of the environmental challenges the building sector is facing, wood is no longer disregarded as outmoded, somewhat nostalgic and rooted in the past, but increasingly understood as one of the most promising building materials for the future. Indeed, there are hardly any other materials that can rival wood's environmental virtues. Wood grows as the biological tissue of trees. This process is mainly powered by solar energy during photosynthesis, which also transforms carbon dioxide into oxygen. Thus wood holds a very low level of embodied energy[6] together with a positive carbon footprint,[7] even if today's heavily industrial wood processing is taken into account.[8] For example, the production of a panel of a given compressive strength in wood requires 500 times less energy than in steel.[9] Thus wood is one of the very few highly energy-efficient, naturally renewable and fully recyclable building materials we currently have at our disposal.

In addition to the ecological incentive, the intricate make-up and complex behaviour of wood provides another reason for employing computation to explore its materially inherent design opportunities. In contrast to most other building materials, wood grows as a functional plant material, serving as a tree's load-bearing structure and metabolic infrastructure. Responding to these biological requirements, wood has evolved as a differentiated fibrous, cellular tissue. Its material structure, resulting from evolutionary development and individual growth, is profoundly different to most other construction materials; for example, because glass and steel are specifically designed and industrially produced to satisfy the demands of the building sector, they typically are homogeneous, which means uniform in composition, and isotropic, having identical or very similar properties in all directions. In comparison, wood is heterogeneous, anisotropic and subject to natural irregularities and considerable biological variability.[10]

While wood's intricate structure and related complex behaviour has proven to be a design challenge in the recent past, computational processes allow for a renewed appreciation of the amazing anatomical differentiation, surprising behavioural capacities and related rich design opportunities inherent in it. Thus, the design research projects illustrated here all began with an investigation of the material structure on the microscopic scale.

All trees are vascular, perennial plants that produce tissue through both linear growth on the tips of twigs and thickness growth of the stem.[11] The reproductive tissue for thickness growth – the cambium – is a very thin layer of cells located behind the bark. Through cell division, cambial cells split to produce a new cambial cell and yet another cell that, depending on its location, develops as either a new bark or wood cell. When a wood cell has grown to its final size and shape, the inner surface of its initially fragile primary cell wall becomes stabilised by a considerably stronger and thicker secondary cell wall. The cell walls are mainly composed of layers of a cellulosic structure

On the one hand, to the formed or formable matter we must add an entire energetic materiality in movement, carrying singularities or haecceities that are already like implicit forms that are topological, rather than geometrical, and that combine with processes of deformation: for example, the variable undulations and torsions of the fibers guiding the operation of splitting wood. On the other hand, to the essential properties of the matter deriving from the formal essence we must add variable intensive affects, now resulting from the operation, now on the contrary making it possible: for example, wood that

is more or less porous, more or less elastic and resistant. At any rate, it is a question of surrendering to the wood, then following where it leads by connecting operations to a materiality, instead of imposing a form upon a matter.

— *Gilles Deleuze and Félix Guattari*[12]

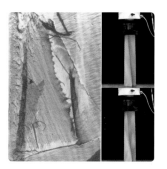

of fibrous-like strands called microfibrils that are reinforced by a matrix of lignin, the constituent that defines woody plants. Especially the middle layer of the secondary cell wall, consisting of densely packed and aligned microfibrils that comprise more than three-quarters of the entire cell wall's composition, has a marked influence on the properties of wood.[13] Consequently, the cell arrangement and the resultant layout of a tree's cellular structure is another critical determinant of wood's behaviour. In softwood, over 90 per cent of the tissue is built up of very long, vertically oriented cells called tracheids, with a much smaller amount of radially oriented ray cells. Hardwood, which is thought to have evolved much later, includes a greater variety of specialised cells, such as vertically oriented tracheids, vessel and fibre cells and also radially oriented ray cells. In both softwood and hardwood, the majority of cells are aligned with the stems axis, accounting for significantly different properties depending on grain direction.[14]

Material Design Research 01: Activating Anisotropy

The anisotropic characteristics of wood resulting from the distribution and orientation of cells can be understood as orientation dependent, variable strength and stiffness,[15] interesting properties that more homogeneous and isotropic materials simply cannot offer. How such wood-specific behavioural features can be integrated in computational design and explored to derive a material-specific gestalt has been examined through various research projects.[16] A number of these projects have investigated how the differential stiffness of wood can be utilised in the development of lightweight compressive surface systems. Due to its highly directional cell structure, the modulus of elasticity of quarter-sawn spruce perpendicular to the grain is 15 times lower than parallel to the grain. The related relative ease of bending a piece in the horizontal plane while maintaining high stiffness in the vertical plane is exploited in the definition of a simple four-sided upright element, which is also equipped with an inner tensile veneer membrane.

Comparative studies with identically shaped metal elements corroborated that this is a truly wood-specific system element, as only the anisotropic properties afford a very simple forming process combined with a high load-bearing capacity in relation to minimal self-weight, which was verified by structural tests. Interestingly, these tests also demonstrated that, when exposed to compressive load, the wood elements show torsional buckling behaviour, whereas the metal counterparts simply buckle. This rotational movement in response to the acting force is caused by the microfibrils in the dominant middle layer of the secondary cell wall, as they are not entirely parallel to the vertical axis but packed in a spiral-like arrangement with a pitch of approximately 15 degrees.

Based on this observation of the intricate relation between material anatomy and behaviour through physical tests, a computational design method was developed that aligns the microfibril angle with the mean force vectors through individual geometric changes to the digitally fabricated parts making up the element. Aligning the material's microscopic structure with the system's macroscopic morphology, the computational process allows exploring larger system configurations of multiple elements. In the resultant lightweight system all elements are arranged in response to the reciprocal relation between material behaviour and acting forces, leading to a versatile and distinctive, yet straightforward to fabricate, material gestalt.

Material Design Research 02: Employing Elasticity

Wood is regularly described as a natural-fibre composite. Lignin and hemicelluloses can be seen as a 'matrix' that is reinforced by the cellulosic microfibrils functioning like 'fibres'. In addition to the aforementioned anisotropy, wood shares a number of properties with synthetic composites, such as glass-fibre-reinforced plastics, characterised by relatively high strain at failure; that is, relatively low stiffness combined with relatively high structural capacity. These material properties lend themselves to construction techniques based on the bending of

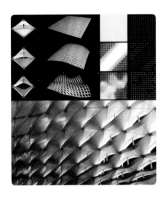

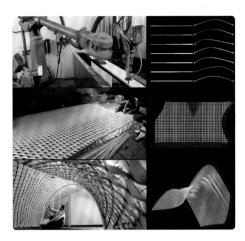

Jian Huang and Minhwan Park, Differentiated Wood Lattice Shell, Performative Wood Studio (Achim Menges), Harvard University Graduate School of Design (GSD), Cambridge, Massachusetts, 2009
A stressed veneer skin was developed to gradually force a wooden lattice into its structurally stable, double-curved state. Based on detailed studies of the achievable actuation force and related element variables such as size, thickness and fibre orientation, actuator locations and required torque, a computational tool for deriving the related actuation protocol was developed and tested in a full-scale prototype.

A digitally controlled robotic water-jet cutting technique allows for gradually reducing the cross section of wooden lathes without damage to the perimeter fibres. Through the related fabrication variables, an entire catalogue of possible bending behaviour can be achieved (top). The fabrication data for constructing the initially planar grid (centre) is derived through a computational design tool for form-finding the lattice shape (bottom). Once the skin actuators are adjusted according to the computationally derived protocol, the lattice rises into its computationally defined, structurally stable double-curved form.

wood, which is a traditional woodworking technique.[17]

Compared to other subtractive or additive fabrication processes, this forming technique offers a number of advantages: it enables the construction of complex, lightweight systems from initially simple planar elements, as it allows for reorienting the grain direction to follow an element's curvature, avoiding excessive fibre run-out on the edges and cross-grain weaknesses.

A series of projects at the University of Stuttgart's Institute for Computational Design (ICD) and at Harvard University Graduate School of Design (GSD) have researched how the bending behaviour of wood can be integrated as a generative driver in computational design, and how today wood can be physically programmed to perform more variable and differentiated bending figures through additional, digitally controlled fabrication techniques.[18] One project aimed at advancing wooden grid shells. These lightweight systems are constructed as initially planar lattices that are subsequently either hoisted or lowered at strategic points to form a double-curved surface structure. Until now, the geometry of grid shells has been based on the bending behaviour of elements with a uniform cross section. In this project, a digitally controlled robotic water-jet cutting technique allows for gradually reducing the cross section of the wooden lathes without damage to the perimeter fibres. Through the related fabrication variables, an entire catalogue of possible bending behaviour can be achieved and embedded in a computational design tool for finding the lattice shape as an equilibrium state of the differentially bent members.

A locally actuated, stressed wooden skin was developed to erect the initially flat lattice. Based on synchronous physical and computational studies and the related encoding of material characteristics and system behaviour, a computational design tool was developed for deriving robotic fabrication and actuation data, and tested in a full-scale prototype. The robotically fabricated members with varying cross sections, together with the laser-cut skin elements with specific grain orientation, are assembled as a flat lattice, but once the actuators are adjusted according

to the computationally derived protocol, the lattice rises into its computationally defined, structurally stable, double-curved form. In the resulting structure, the differentiated transparency and articulation of the skin registers the embedded forces, which maintain equilibrium in the very thin, non-uniformly bent elastic lattice.

As an alternative to the parallel-to-grain manipulations through robotic water-jet slicing investigated in this undertaking, another project investigated cross-grain manipulations through robotic kerfing. In order to achieve more elaborate and controlled bending and warping figures, the precise control of gradual variations of kerf depth, length, frequency and orientation through a six-axis industrial robot equipped with a circular saw blade were physically studied and integrated in the computational design tool development. The resultant custom-programmed application provides a computational form-finding tool for the overall system, generates the individual kerf patterns that condition the physical forming behaviour of each element, and outputs the relevant geometric data directly in robot control code. This enabled the immediate fabrication of the individually kerfed white-oak slats that were subsequently pre-stressed, joined into components and assembled as a 5-metre (16.4-foot) tall hyperboloid prototype.

In addition to these subtractive techniques, a wide range of additive fabrication techniques such as differentiated vacuum lamination and even biochemical manipulations of the elastic bending behaviour have been explored in various other research projects, some of which are also illustrated here. The feasibility of using the elastic bending behaviour of wood as a generative driver in the computational design process for construction-scale structures was demonstrated through the ICD/ITKE Research Pavilion at the University of Stuttgart in 2010 (see pp 44-51). Similarly, the Responsive Surface Structure and Hygroscopic Envelopes projects at the Department for Form Generation and Materialisation at HFG Offenbach and the ICD at Stuttgart were dedicated to researching how wood's hygroscopic behaviour

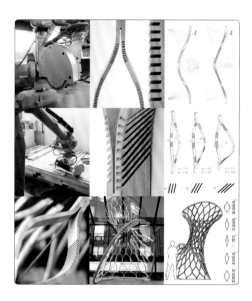

Brad Crane, Andrew McGee, Marshall Prado and Yang Zhao, Kerf-Based Complex Wood Systems, Performative Wood Studio (Achim Menges), Harvard University Graduate School of Design (GSD), Cambridge, Massachusetts, 2010
This project investigates the possibility of programming the elastic bending behaviour of pre-steamed, white-oak slats by locally differentiated kerfs. In order to construct a full-scale hyperboloid prototype, the material properties of white oak, the process variables of wood bending and the fabrication parameters of a six-axis industrial robot equipped with a circular saw blade were integrated in a custom-programmed design tool.

Timothee Boitouzet, Constantine Bouras and Francisco Izquierdo, Meta-Wood, Performative Wood Studio (Achim Menges), Harvard University Graduate School of Design (GSD), Cambridge, Massachusetts, 2010
Biochemical manipulations can be employed to programme the elastic bending behaviour of wood, allowing for much smaller bending radii.

can be utilised in the design of environmentally responsive systems (see pp 52–9).

Material Design Research 03: Instrumentalising Irregularity

All of the research projects introduced above employ material capacities rooted in the microscopic structure of wood to inform computational design processes operating at the macrolevel of the material system. However, the scale range of design can now also be extended towards intervening at the microscopic level of the material itself, as demonstrated by the Microstructural Manipulations research undertaking conducted at Harvard GSD.[19] This project commenced with the development of an undulated, lightweight compressive surface structure to be constructed from long strips of quarter-sawn pine veneer. Initial tests indicated that the majority of the system's compressive strength can be ascribed to the more robust 'latewood' cell regions, leading to the hypothesis that the 'earlywood' could be partially removed without a significant effect on the overall structural capacity.

The terms 'earlywood' and 'latewood' refer to the different regions of tissue produced within one seasonal cycle. In climates with considerable seasonal changes, the latewood features significantly thicker cell walls and much denser cell arrangement than earlywood, resulting in pronounced transverse annual growth rings and distinct longitudinal grain. Following the initial hypothesis, the aim was to strategically eliminate structurally dispensable earlywood regions with a precise laser-cutter. This highlighted the fact that wood is always subject to natural irregularities and biological variability, as no two pieces of wood are exactly alike. Thus a computational design process based on a continuous information flow from scanning the individual anatomical features of each wood piece to the eventual digital fabrication was developed.

First, a finite element (FE) structural analysis of the overall system is conducted and all wood elements intended for construction digitised on a purpose-built scanner. An algorithmic procedure then isolates the earlywood and latewood regions, comparing this data with the structural analysis data and determining, depending on stress intensity, the cut pattern for a laser that subsequently erases the dispensable earlywood. This fully automated and rapid process results in remarkable patterns of removed earlywood, which are specific to the individual anatomy and significantly reduce the system's mass while only having a marginal effect on the load-bearing capacity. More importantly, the project breaks first ground in developing design processes capable of registering and utilising the unique anatomical features of wood through an information feedback from material scan to computational design, analysis and digital fabrication, enabling an understanding of wood as a naturally grown, high-performance composite material.

Those who consider the above as far-fetched and improbable may wish to consider the following. Log-scanning technology is already in place in many advanced sawmills,[20] where X-ray tomography is used to produce information about log morphology, grain structure and anatomical features. This technology is currently used to identify irregularities or 'defects' in a log, to algorithmically determine its most profitable breakdown,[21] and to control the cutting-up process by steering the head saw. The by-product is a comprehensive anatomical data set of all individual wood pieces produced. However, until now this material information has been lost once the wood leaves the sawmill. Employing these already existing anatomical datasets in an integrated computational design and fabrication process may be the next step towards (re)discovering the complex capacities and biological variability of wood within a truly material practice of architecture. ᗡ

Institute for Computational Design (Achim Menges) and Institute of Building Structures and Structural Design (Jan Knippers), ICD/ITKE Research Pavilion 2010, University of Stuttgart, Stuttgart, 2010
Based on the elastic bending behaviour of birch-plywood lamellas, this project developed a novel bending-active structure by combining contemporary means of materially informed computational design, advanced engineering simulation and robotic manufacturing.

Jose Ahedo, Microstructural Manipulations, Performative Wood Studio (Achim Menges), Harvard University Graduate School of Design (GSD), Cambridge, Massachusetts, 2009
below: The terms 'earlywood' and 'latewood' refer to the different regions of tissue produced within one seasonal cycle. In climates with considerable seasonal changes, the latewood features significantly thicker cell walls and much denser cell arrangement than earlywood, resulting in pronounced grain (top). Based on the scanning data of all wood elements intended for construction (A), an algorithmic procedure isolates the earlywood and latewood regions (B), compares this data with the structural analysis data (C), and determines, depending on stress intensity (D), the cut pattern for a laser (E) that subsequently erases the dispensable earlywood (F).

Based on the individual anatomy of each scanned piece of veneer, an integrated process of material scan, computational design, analysis and digital fabrication allows grain-specific micro manipulations limited to earlywood regions and thus allows for related anatomy-specific modulation of wood's macroscopic behaviour.

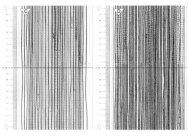

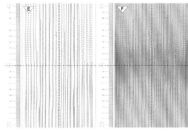

Notes
1. Rob Howard, *Computing in Construction: Pioneers and the Future*, Butterworth-Heinemann (Oxford/Woburn), 1998. Interesting early examples of generative design applications are GRASP (generation of random access site plans) or RUMOR (random generation and evaluation of plans) developed by Eric Teicholz at the Harvard Laboratory for Computer Graphics in the 1960s.
2. Achim Menges, 'Form Generation and Materialization at the Transition from Computer-aided to Computational Design', *Detail*, Vol 2010, No 04, 2010, pp 330–5.
3. Manuel DeLanda, 'Philosophies of Design: The Case of Modelling Software', in Jaime Salazar (ed), *Verb Processing*, Actar (Barcelona), 2001, p 132.
4. Achim Menges, 'Integral Formation and Materialisation: Computational Form and Material Gestalt', in B Kolarevic and K Klinger (eds), *Manufacturing Material Effects: Rethinking Design and Making in Architecture*, Routledge (New York), 2008, pp 195–210.
5. Michael Hensel and Achim Menges, 'Form- und Materialwerdung: Das Konzept der Materialsysteme', *ArchPlus*, No 188, 2008, pp 18–25.
6. A Alcorn, *Embodied Energy Coefficients of Building Materials*, Centre for Building Performance Research (Wellington), 1996, p 92.
7. Josef Kolb, *Systems in Timber Engineering: Loadbearing Structures and Component Layers*, Birkhäuser (Basel), 2008, p 19.
8. Dirk Scheer, Andreas Feil and Carolin Zerwer, *Nachhaltigkeit im Bereich Bauen und Wohnen – ökologische Bewertung der Bauholz-Kette*, Institut für ökologische Wirtschaftsforschung (Heidelberg), 2006.
9. JE Gordon, *Structures*, Da Capo Press (Cambridge, MA), 2003, p 322.
10. RB Hoadley, *Understanding Wood*, Taunton Press (Newton, CT), 2000.
11. Rudi Wagenführ, *Anatomie des Holzes*, Drw Verlag (Leinfelden-Echterdingen), 1999.
12. Gilles Deleuze and Félix Guattari. *A Thousand Plateaus*, trans Brian Massumi, University of Minnesota Press (Minneapolis), 1987, p 408.

13. John M Dinwoodie, *Timber: Its Nature and Behaviour*, E&F Spon Press (London), 2000.
14. John R Barnett and George Jeronimidis (eds), *Wood Quality and its Biological Basis*, Blackwell CRC Press (Oxford), 2003.
15. Andre Wagenführ, *Die strukturelle Anisotropie von Holz als Chance für technische Innovationen*, Hirzel Verlag (Stuttgart), 2008.
16. Achim Menges, 'Performative Wood: Integral Computational Design for Timber Construction', in *Reform: Building a Better Tomorrow, Proceedings of the 29th Conference of the Association For Computer Aided Design In Architecture (ACADIA)*, Chicago, 21–25 October 2009, pp 66–74.
17. L Schleining, *The Complete Manual of Wood Bending*, Linden Publishing (Fresno, CA), 2001.
18. Achim Menges, 'Integrative Design Computation: Integrating Material Behaviour and Robotic Manufacturing Processes in Computational Design for Performative Wood Constructions', in *Integration Through Computation, Proceedings of the 31st Conference of the Association For Computer Aided Design In Architecture (ACADIA)*, Calgary, 13–16 October 2011.
19. Achim Menges, 'Material Information: Integrating Material Characteristics and Behavior in Computational Design for Performative Wood Construction', in *Life In:Formation, Proceedings of the 30th Conference of the Association For Computer Aided Design In Architecture (ACADIA)*, New York City, 21–24 October 2010, pp 151–8.
20. Erol Sarigul, A Lynn Abbott and Daniel L Schmoldt, 'Rule-Driven Defect Detection in CT Images of Hardwood Logs', *Journal for Computers and Electronics in Agriculture*, Vol 41 (1–3), 2003, pp 101–19.
21. Alfred Rinnhofer, Alexander Petutschniggb and Jean-Philippe Andreua, 'Internal Log Scanning for Optimizing Breakdown', *Journal for Computers and Electronics in Agriculture*, Vol 41 (1–3), 2003, pp 7–21.

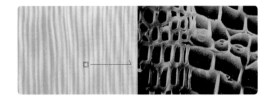

Moritz Fleischmann, Jan Knippers,
Julian Lienhard, Achim Menges
and Simon Schleicher

Institute for Computational Design (Achim Menges) and Institute of Building Structures and Structural Design (Jan Knippers), ICD/ITKE Research Pavilion 2010, University of Stuttgart, Stuttgart, 2010
Through the integration of computational design, advanced simulation and robotic fabrication, the ICD/ITKE Research Pavilion 2010 aims at further developing the lineage of bending-active structures.

MATERIAL BEHAVIOUR

EMBEDDING PHYSICAL PROPERTIES IN COMPUTATIONAL DESIGN PROCESSES

Material behaviour computes form. In the physical world, material form is always inseparably connected to internal constraints and external forces; in the virtual space of digital design, though, form and force are usually treated as separate entities – divided into processes of geometric form generation and subsequent engineering simulation. Using the example of the interdisciplinary ICD/ITKE Research Pavilion, constructed at the University of Stuttgart in 2010, **Moritz Fleischmann, Jan Knippers, Julian Lienhard, Achim Menges and Simon Schleicher** explain how feedback between computational design, advanced simulation and robotic fabrication expands the design space towards previously unexplored architectural possibilities.

The ICD/ITKE Research Pavilion 2010, an experimental bending-active structure, is located at the city campus of the University of Stuttgart.

Design computation provides the possibilities of integrating physical properties and material behaviour as generative drivers in the architectural design process.[1] Thus architectural form, material formation and structural performance can be considered synchronously. While in most architectural design approaches a scheme is conceived and drawn, modelled or even digitally generated as a construct of geometrically described, inert parts, in computational design material elements can be defined by behaviour rather than shape.[2] Thus larger assemblies can be explored and derived from the interaction of such behavioural elements and external data, and understood as contributing to an overall performative capacity. Here, the design space is defined and constrained by material behaviour and its possible modulations through variations in production and fabrication. Far beyond standardised building systems and well-established structural typologies, unknown points in the design space can be explored by employing design computation as a calibration between the virtual processes of generating form and the physical becoming of material gestalt.[3] In reciprocity with defined design parameters, material behaviour unleashes its capacity to generate, organise and structure: material computes.

How can one imagine architectural computational design processes that enable material behaviour to become an active driver in the generation of form, structure and space? As a vehicle for providing an insight and critical reflection on the related design methods, a collaborative research undertaking conducted by the Institute for Computational Design (ICD) and the Institute of Building Structures and Structural Design (ITKE) at the University of Stuttgart is explained below. The ICD/ITKE Research Pavilion 2010[4] project is based on a common material behaviour: elastic bending. The typical axis curve of a pin-supported linear element in the post-buckled state when deformed within the elastic range of a material is known as the 'elastica curve'.[5] The research project indicates how even a relatively simple behaviour such as elastic bending can lead to novel design possibilities of bending-active systems[6] that are surprisingly versatile, complex and structurally effective.

Due to the considerable technical and intellectual challenges of integrating material behaviour in the design process, only very few examples of bending-active architectures exist. It may not come as a surprise that vernacular architecture, with its more immediate relation to material characteristics and behaviour, has recognised and utilised the structural capacity of elastically bent structures for a long time. For example, the Madan people in southern Iraq have developed a profound understanding of the material behaviour of bundled reed.[7] Their Mudhif houses are built out of conical, initially straight reed bundles

that are fixed to the ground and subsequently
connected at the tips to form elastically
bent arch structures.[8] In addition to these
culturally evolved vernacular architectures, a
few examples of technologically developed,
bending-active structures exist, such as the
Hooke Park workshop building in Dorset,
UK (1989) by ABK Architects, Frei Otto and
Buro Happold. Here, the primary structure
uses elastically bent, green round-wood poles
provided by local spruce thinnings, which are
usually considered unsuitable for construction.
Multiple relatively thin poles were connected
to create longer elements that were fixed to
the ground and connected at the top to form
a series of varying arches.[9] In this case, the
bending behaviour of the poles was calibrated
with a physical hanging chain design model,
an adequate method because the elastica
curve of bent linear elements and the catenary
curve of hanging chains are very similar within
a specific shape range.[10]

The ICD/ITKE Research Pavilion aimed
at further developing this unsung lineage
of bending-active structures, exploring their
architectural potential through contemporary
means of computational design, engineering
simulation and robotic manufacturing. This
entailed the advance of computational design
processes by embedding system-specific
physical properties and material behaviour,
calibrating these with finite element methods
(FEMs) for simulations, employing a six-axis
industrial robot for fabrication and utilising
material behaviour as the actual construction
technique on site for achieving a complex
morphology from initially entirely planar

plywood. The methodological advances also
allowed seeking innovation on the material
system level, especially in regards to two
aspects: first, the project aimed for integrating
skin and structure in one mono-material,
bending-active system without the need for
other constructional elements; second, and in
contrast to the aforementioned projects, here
the elastic bending behaviour is not employed
to generate the global shape and structure of
the systems, but rather to define a series of
behavioural components that spatially mediate
an intricate network of forces. This also has
profound ramifications on the methodological
level: different to other form-finding processes
for form-active structures, the multiplicity
of system-defining parameters and their
extended variable ranges ensure a truly open,
exploratory design process of computational
form generation rather than a deterministic
process of analytical form-finding only. The
result is a novel bending-active structure, an
intricate network of joint points and related
force vectors that are spatially mediated by
the elasticity of thin plywood lamellas.[11]
The research pavilion's structure is entirely
based on the bending deformation of thin
birch plywood strips within the elastic range.

Institute for Computational Design (Achim Menges) and Institute of
Building Structures and Structural Design (Jan Knippers), ICD/ITKE
Research Pavilion 2010, University of Stuttgart, Stuttgart, 2010
bottom: The material investigation commenced with physically
testing the elastic behaviour of thin plywood strips and calibrating the
results with finite element method (FEM) simulations. Based on these
experiments, the material behaviour of the plywood elements is encoded
in a generative computational design tool.

The irregularly oscillating distribution of strip connection points
prevents the local weak spots of reduced effective depth at the
joints from impacting on the global system. The computationally
derived distribution pattern results in a stable equilibrium state and
a distinctive articulation of the structural envelope.

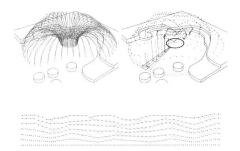

Similar to synthetic composites, such as glass-fibre-reinforced plastic, wood as a natural fibre composite shows relatively high strain at failure, which means high load-bearing capacity with relatively low stiffness.[12] These material properties and related behaviour are especially well suited for construction techniques that employ the elastic bending of wood in order to form complex, lightweight structures from initially simple, planar building elements.

The design of the prototype pavilion began with the development of a computational design tool. In this tool all relevant material behavioural characteristics are integrated as parametric dependencies based on a large number of physical and computational tests. The tests focused on measuring the deflections of elastically bent plywood strips in relation to various specification parameters as well as the calibration and corroboration of the resulting data with FEMs. The developed integrative computational tool generated possible system morphologies together with all relevant geometric information and directly outputted the data required for both subsequent FEM simulations and the manufacturing with a six-axis industrial robot.

The plywood strips are robotically manufactured as planar elements, and subsequently connected so that elastically bent and tensioned regions alternate along their length. The force that is locally stored in each bent region of the strip, and maintained by the corresponding tensioned region of the neighbouring strip, greatly increases the structural stiffness of the self-equilibrating system. This is explained by the fact that the bent arch induces tensile stress into the straight arch. This tension pre-stress increases the lateral stiffness of the straight arch and hence the geometrical stiffness of the entire system. In order to prevent local points of reduced effective depth, the locations of the joints between strips need to oscillate along the structure, resulting in a distinct articulation of the envelope. Introducing irregularity in the overall structure allows a stable global system to be achieved despite the system's inherent local weak spots. As a consequence of this strategy several hundred geometrically different parts needed to be fabricated. So, in addition to the material behaviour, the manufacturing and assembly logics were integrated in the computational process. Based on the machine constraints of the six-axis fabrication robot to be used, the three critical details of the system were developed: 1) the shear-resistant joint for connecting adjacent strips; 2) the tension puzzle joint to connect strip segments of limited stock size; and 3) the joint between elastic strip and the structural base. The direct generation of all manufacturing data allowed the rapid fabrication of 500 geometrically unique parts.

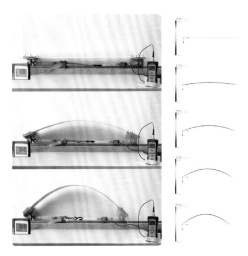
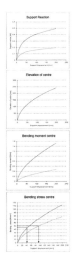

Based on the planar strip configuration
and definition of connection points it is
possible to simulate the erection process
and thereby the residual stress in a finite
element-based simulation. The form-found
structural analysis model allows verification
of the geometrical shape, including its
residual stress, as well as analysis of
the deformations and stress levels under
external wind loads.

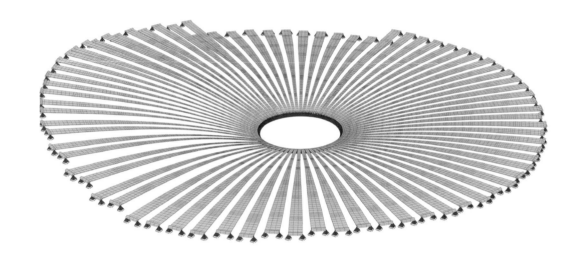

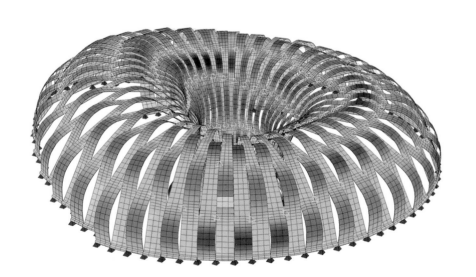

Through integrative computational design
processes, the basic system behaviour (top:
FEM simulation) is developed towards a
constructional material system based on
the characteristics of the employed robotic
manufacturing processes (bottom: 3-D
computational detailing).

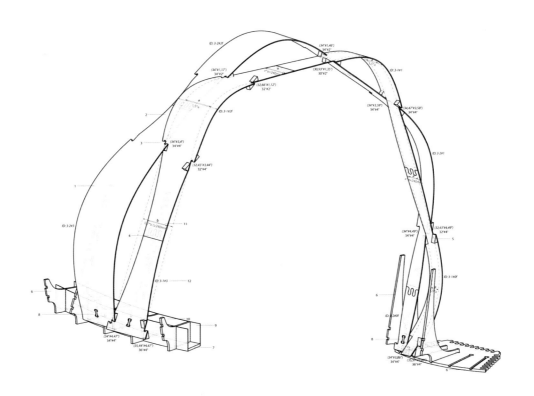

The combination of the pre-stress resulting from
the elastic bending during the assembly process
and the morphological differentiation of the
joint locations enables a very lightweight and
materially efficient system. The entire pavilion
was constructed using only 6.5-millimetre (¼-
inch) thin birch plywood sheets.

Robotic fabrication allows the fabrication of
500 geometrical unique parts with only three
types of connection details and about 1,500
different angle set-ups (below left). On site, the
material behaviour computes the shape of the
pavilion (right). The planar strips simply need to
be connected and then automatically find their
specific shape.

In contrast to the substantial intellectual investment in developing the design computation and simulation processes, and the relatively involving task of programming the robot, the assembly process was straightforward and quick to execute, with no need for extensive scaffolding or additional equipment as the planar strips simply needed to be connected and then automatically found their specific shape. In other words, on site the material behaviour itself computes the shape of the pavilion.

The combination of the pre-stress resulting from the elastic bending during the assembly process and the morphological differentiation of the joint locations enabled a very lightweight and materially efficient system. The entire pavilion was constructed using only 6.5-millimetre (¼-inch) thin birch plywood sheets. This extremely thin and materially efficient skin was at the same time the load-bearing structure as well as the light-modulating and weather-protecting envelope for the semi-interior extension of the public square.

The spatial articulation and structural system was based on a half-torus shape. Defining the urban edge of the university campus, it touched the ground topography that provided seating opportunities on the street-facing corner. In contrast to this, the torus side that faced the public square was lifted from the ground to form a free-spanning opening. Inside, the toroidal space could never be perceived in its entirety, leading to a surprising spatial depth that was further enhanced by the sequence of direct and indirect illumination resulting from the convex and concave undulations of the envelope, which found its form as the equilibrium state of the embedded forces.

Beyond the investigation of the related architectural qualities, the construction of the research project allowed verification of the presented computational design approach by comparing the computational design model, the related FEM model and the actual geometry of the constructed pavilion. In collaboration with geodesic engineers, the constructed pavilion was repeatedly digitised using full-scale scanning and geodesic measurement techniques resulting in a point-cloud data set. Comparing the results of the generative computational design process with FEM simulations and the exact measurement of the geometry that the material 'computed' on site indicates that the suggested integration of design computation and materialisation is no longer an idealised goal but a feasible proposition.[13]

The project demonstrates how focusing the computational design process on material behaviour rather than geometric shape allows for unfolding performative capacity and material resourcefulness while at the same time expanding the design space towards hitherto unexplored architectural possibilities. The synthesis of material, form and performance enables a complex structure to be unfolded from an uncomplicated system. The pavilion's equilibrium state unfolds a unique architectural space while at the same time being extremely efficient with the employed material resources. ⌂

bottom: In order to verify the computational design research, the geometry the material behaviour 'computed' on site was scanned with the help of geodesic engineers from the IIGS University of Stuttgart (top left), resulting in a comprehensive 3-D data set of the entire structure (top right). Comparing the computational design model (centre left), the manufacturing data model (bottom left), the FEM simulation model (centre right) and the 3-D scan data of the geometry as constructed on-site (bottom right) demonstrates that the suggested integration of design computation and materialisation is no longer an idealised goal but a feasible proposition.

Inside the pavilion, the toroidal space can never be perceived in its entirety, leading to a surprising spatial depth that is further enhanced by the sequence of convex and concave undulations of the envelope.

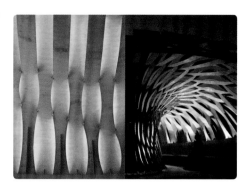

Notes

1. At the intersection of architectural design and structural engineering, as in the work of Frei Otto and Heinz Isler among many others, numerous examples of employing physical behaviour in so-called form-finding processes already exist. What is proposed here is: 1) extending form-finding towards form-generation by a full integration of computational design, structural simulation and robotic fabrication; and 2) developing methods for employing material behaviour in the construction process itself, rather than using it for abstracted design models only.
2. Achim Menges, 'Pluripotent Components: An Alternative Approach to Parametric Design', *AA Files No 52*, AA Publications (London), 2005, pp 63–74.
3. Achim Menges, 'Integral Formation and Materialisation: Computational Form and Material Gestalt', in B Kolarevic and K Klinger (eds), *Manufacturing Material Effects: Rethinking Design and Making in Architecture*, Routledge (New York), 2008, pp 195–210.
4. ICD/ITKE Research Pavilion 2010: ICD (A Menges) and ITKE (J Knippers), M Fleischmann, S Schleicher, C Robeller, J Lienhard, D D'Souza, K Dierichs, A Eisenhardt, M Vollrath, K Wächter, T Irowetz, OD Krieg, Á Mahmutovic, P Meschendörfer, L Möhler, M Pelzer, K Zerbe.
5. Raph Levien, *The Elastica: A Mathematical History*, University of California (Berkeley, CA), 2008.
6. Jan Knippers, Jan Cremers, Markus Gabler and Julian Lienhard, *Construction Manual for Polymers + Membranes*, Edition Detail (Munich), 2011, p 134. The term bending-active was introduced by the authors to describe curved-beam or surface structures that base their geometry on the elastic deformation of initially straight or planar elements.
7. Klaus Dunkelberg, *IL 31 Bambus – Bamboo*, Karl Krämer Verlag (Stuttgart), 1985.
8. Paul Oliver, *Dwellings: The Vernacular House World Wide*, Phaidon Press (London), 2003, p 122.
9. Michael Hensel and Achim Menges, 'Holz Form Findung', *ArchPlus*, No 193, 2009, pp 106–9.
10. Jürgen Hennicke, *IL 10 Gitterschalen: Grid Shells*, Karl Krämer Verlag (Stuttgart), 1975, p 35. See also Edward Allen and Waclaw Zalewski, *Form and Forces: Designing Efficient, Expressive Structures*, John Wiley & Sons (London), 2010, p 67.
11. Julian Lienhard, Simon Schleicher and Jan Knippers, 'Bending-Active Structures: Research Pavilion ICD/ITKE', in D Nethercot and S Pellegrino et al (eds), *Proceedings of the International Symposium of the IABSE-IASS Symposium, Taller Longer Lighter*, London, 2011.
12. André Wagenführ and Frieder Scholz, *Taschenbuch der Holztechnik*, Carl Hanser Verlag (Munich), 2008, p 122.
13. Achim Menges, Moritz Fleischmann, Simon Schleicher, 'ICD/ITKE Research Pavilion', in Ruairi Glynn and Bob Sheil (eds), *Fabricate: Making Digital Architecture*, Riverside Architectural Press (Waterloo, ON), 2011.

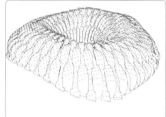

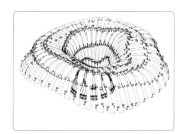

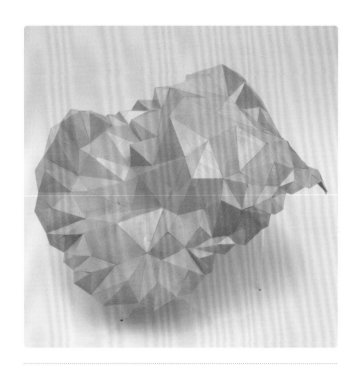

Steffen Reichert and Achim Menges,
Responsive Surface Structure II,
Department for Form Generation and
Materialisation, HFG Offenbach, Offenbach
am Main, Germany, 2008
Wood's hygroscopic behaviour is the basis
here for simple, moisture-responsive parts
that are in one embedded sensor, with no-
energy motor or regulating element. They
enabled the development of a system that
responds to changes of relative humidity
by opening or closing the surface. As all
the responsive capacity is embedded in
the material itself, no additional technical
equipment or external energy is needed
for the system to react to environmental
changes.

MATERIAL CAPACITY

EMBEDDED RESPONSIVENESS

Most attempts towards climate-responsive architecture rely heavily on elaborate technical equipment superimposed on otherwise inert material constructs. In contrast, natural systems embed all the responsive capacity in the structure of the material itself. In this article, **Achim Menges and Steffen Reichert** present the development of biomimetic responsive material systems that require neither the supply of external energy nor any kind of mechanical or electronic control. They introduce their research on physically programming the humidity-reactive behaviour of these systems, and explain the possibilities this opens up for a strikingly simple yet truly ecologically embedded architecture in constant feedback and interaction with its surrounding environment.

Iva Kremsa, Kenzo Nakakoji and Etien
Santiago, Wood and Hygroscopic
Behaviour, Performative Wood Studio
(Achim Menges), Harvard University
Graduate School of Design (GSD),
Cambridge, Massachusetts, 2009
Conifer cones are biological examples
of moisture-actuated passive systems.
For example, a spruce cone reacts to a
decrease in moisture content by opening
its scales, leading to the release of the
seeds. Interestingly, here even the dead
tissue is capable of repetitive opening
and closing cycles as the humidity
responsiveness is literally ingrained in the
material itself.

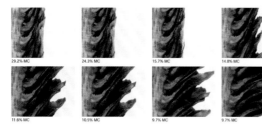

Interaction with, rather than protection from, environmental dynamics is increasingly understood as a critical characteristic of performative architecture. Today climate-responsiveness is typically conceived as a technical function enabled by myriad mechanical and electronic sensing, actuating and regulating devices. In contrast to this superimposition of high-tech equipment on otherwise inert material constructs, nature suggests a fundamentally different, no-tech strategy: in various biological systems the responsive capacity is quite literally ingrained in the material itself. Employing similar design strategies of physically programming material systems rather than equipping them with additional technical devices may enable a shift from a mechanical towards a biological paradigm of climate-responsiveness in architecture.

Natural Systems: Ingrained Responsiveness

Nature has evolved a great variety of dynamic systems interacting with climatic influences. For architecture, one particularly interesting way is the moisture-driven movement that can be observed in some plants. Different to other plant movements produced by active cell pressure changes, as in the well-known example of the Venus flytrap,[1] this movement consists of a passive response to humidity changes. It does not require any sensory system or motor function. It is independent from the metabolism and does not consume any energy. The responsive capacity is ingrained in the material's hygroscopic behaviour and anisotropic characteristics. Anisotropy denotes the directional dependence of a material's characteristics as, for example, the different physical properties of wood in relation to grain directionality. Hygroscopicity refers to a substance's ability to take in moisture from the atmosphere when dry and yield moisture to the atmosphere when wet, thereby maintaining a moisture content in equilibrium with the surrounding relative humidity. In this process of adsorption and desorption the material changes physically, as water molecules become bonded to the material molecules.

An interesting example previously encountered as being of particular relevance for architecture is the hygroscopic behaviour of conifer cones enabled by their anisotropic material characteristics.[2] These cones are organs bearing the reproductive structures of coniferous plants (*Pinophyta*), most commonly known in the form of spruce or pine cones. The seeds contained within the cones are released by opening the scales. At this point the cell tissue of a mature cone is already dead, yet still capable of performing many opening and closing cycles. As this movement is rooted in the material's intrinsic capacity to interact with the external environment, even the no-longer living tissue still operates. Thus conifer cones provide an interesting example of how structured tissue can passively respond to environmental stimuli, as the cone scales react to changes in relative humidity.

The cone opening (when dried) and closing (when wetted) is enabled by the bilayered structure of the scales' material. The outer layer, consisting of parallel, long and densely packed thick-walled cells, hygroscopically reacts to an increase or decrease of relative humidity by expanding or contracting, while the inner layer remains relatively stable.[3] The resultant differential dimensional change of the layers translates into a shape change of the scale, causing the cone's overall opening and closing movement.[4] Instrumentalising hygroscopic material behaviour in this way is especially promising in architecture. In contrast to most other modes of actuating material systems, it requires neither supply of external energy nor any kind of mechanical or electronic control. All the responsive capacity is embedded in the structure of the material itself.

Performative Wood: Instrumental Hygroscopicity

The research on humidity-responsive hygroscopically actuated architectural systems at the Department for Form Generation and Materialisation at HFG Offenbach and the Institute for Computational Design (ICD) at the University of Stuttgart commenced with the development of reactive bilayered material elements based on the principle of conifer cones. Similar to the cones, the hygroscopicity and anisotropy innate to wooden material was to achieve this, but in combination with a synthetic composite. Teasing out wood's responsive capacity in this way requires an in-depth understanding of the reciprocities between the anatomy of wood, its behavioural characteristics and its interaction with environmental dynamics. So how is wood hygroscopic?

Wood is a cellular structure. The cell walls, which constitute the actual wood tissue and in most cases enclose an inner cavity called the cell lumen, consist of a natural fibre composite[5] that can be thought of as principally quite similar to the technical composite we all are familiar with, such as glass-fibre-reinforced plastics. In wood, cellulose, or more specifically cellulosic microfibrils, are attributed the role of the 'fibres' that are embedded in a 'matrix' of hemicelluloses and lignin.[6] Wood is hygroscopic because water can be adsorbed and chemically bonded to the cellulose and hemicelluloses on a molecular level. This water adsorbed within the cell wall is called bound water, as opposed to free water contained in the cell lumen. The free water has hardly any effect on the dimensional behaviour of wood. In contrast, the removal of bound water (desorption) reduces the distance between the microfibrils in the cell tissue, resulting in both a substantial increase in strength due to interfibrillar bonding and a significant decrease in overall dimension. Interestingly, these changes are fully reversible.[7] This is why the pine cone can open and close over and over again, even long after its biological function of releasing the seeds has been fulfilled. It is physically programmed to do so.

The fibre saturation point refers to the state when the cell wall has reached its maximum capacity to hold bound water while there is no free water in the cell cavities. Beyond this point, the cell lumen begins to fill with free water. Generally, the amount of both bound and free water is referred to as the moisture content. It is expressed as the percentage of the water's weight in relation to the weight of the wood substance in which it is contained. Typically, the fibre saturation point is at around 27 to 30 per cent moisture content. Below this point, two fascinating things happen: first, any change to the bound water content within the cell walls will cause a dimensional change of wood; second, the actual amount of bound water content is a function of the relative humidity and, to a much lesser degree, temperature of the surrounding air. The temporal equilibrium condition reached when the wood neither loses nor gains moisture in exchange with the environment is called equilibrium moisture content. As wood always seeks to reach this equilibrium, it continuously responds to changes in the

Microscopic images of maple
Microscopic photographs of maple show the difference in cell arrangement in the transverse (top), tangential (centre) and radial (bottom) directions leading to a highly anisotropic behaviour when moisture content changes. Swelling and shrinking in the tangential direction is approximately 10 times higher than along the longitudinal axis.

Wood is hygroscopic because water can be adsorbed and chemically bonded to the cellulose and hemicelluloses on a molecular level. This water adsorbed within the cell wall is called bound water, as opposed to free water contained in the cell lumen.

Steffen Reichert, Achim Menges and
Florian Krampe, Hygroscopic Envelopes,
Institute for Computational Design
(ICD), University of Stuttgart, Stuttgart,
2010–11
top: The humidity-responsive veneer-
composite element functions by translating
wood's dimensional changes caused
by varying moisture content into shape
changes. For example, given an increase of
relative humidity from 40 to 70 per cent
the veneer element changes from a straight
to a curved shape. By altering material
and manufacturing parameters, the veneer-
composite elements can be physically
programmed to perform different response
figures in various humidity ranges.

centre: The veneer-composite element can
be used as the basic constituent of a larger
humidity-responsive system. As elaborate
testing has shown, the material system can
be physically programmed to either open
(right sample) or close (left sample) in
response to an increase in relative humidity.

bottom: Elaborate laboratory tests in a
climate chamber demonstrated the material
system's capacity to rapidly respond to
changes in relative humidity (right). When
the relative humidity increases, the system
consistently opens and closes over a large
number of cycles. Literally embodying the
capacity to sense, actuate and regulate, the
surface locally responds to microclimatic
variations (left).

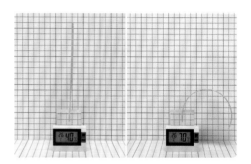

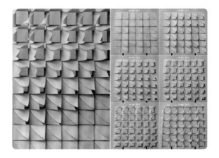

surrounding relative humidity by adjusting the bound water content, resulting in constant dimensional movement.

The anatomy of wood regulates this dimensional movement.[8] More than three-quarters of a wood cell's wall consists of the middle layer of the secondary wall structure, which has been found to largely determine the dimensional movement of wood.[9] As the microfibrils in this dominant wall layer are all oriented at a slight angle to the longitudinal axis of the cell, and as most cells are oriented parallel to the stem axis, the shrinking and swelling of wood is highly anisotropic. Dimensional change along the longitudinal axis (parallel to the grain) of wood is negligible. However, the transverse movement is significant, whereby the dimensional change in the tangential direction (perpendicular to the grain and parallel to the growth rings) is generally greater than in the radial direction (perpendicular to the grain and perpendicular to the growth rings). Depending on grain direction, swelling and shrinking varies from 0.1 per cent (longitudinal) to more than 10 per cent (tangential), an over 100-fold range.

This anisotropic dimensional behaviour was exploited as part of the research at HFG Offenbach and the ICD at Stuttgart in the development of a humidity-responsive veneer-composite element based on simple quarter-cut maple veneer, chosen because of its relatively high tangential dimensional change in combination with a comparatively low modulus of elasticity. A change in relative humidity, for example from 40 to 70 per cent, leads to a rapid dimensional change of the veneer that is translated into a significant shape change of the element. Given a rapid rise in relative humidity, the element changes from the straight to an acutely curved state within a few minutes or less. The veneer-composite element instrumentalises the material's responsive capacity in one surprisingly simple component that is at the same time embedded sensor, no-energy motor and regulating element. Moreover, all veneer-composite elements respond independently. The resultant decentralised control and collective behaviour at the system level is sensitive to local microclimates and at the same time highly robust.

Material System: Programmed Responsiveness

The dimensional change of wood is directly proportional to changes in moisture content. Hence, a specific increase in moisture content will always result in the same swelling or shrinking dimensions of a particular piece of wood. However, in combination with another synthetic composite, this linear dependency can be expanded to achieve highly specific yet diverse shape changes. In other words, the veneer-composite elements can be physically programmed as a material system to perform different response figures in various humidity ranges. For example, the ICD's experiments in a climate chamber have shown the following. Using the same veneer as a starting point, two veneer-composite elements can be produced – one entirely straight and the other acutely curved at a humidity level of 40 per cent. When relative humidity rises to 70 per cent, the initially straight element will change to an acutely curved shape as mentioned above, while the other will become straight. Exposed to the very same environmental changes, the two test pieces geometrically respond in exactly the opposite way.

Such substantially different behaviour can be achieved through specific alterations to the production parameters. The composite system elements can be programmed to materially compute different shapes within variable humidity-response ranges by adjusting the following five parameters: 1) fibre directionality, 2) layout of the natural and synthetic composite, 3) length-width-thickness ratio, 4) geometry of the element, and especially 5) humidity control during the production phase. This enables the development of elements that either open or close when ambient humidity increases, as well as the careful choreography of their response range and behaviour.

The manifold behavioural capacities at the element level open up various possibilities for developments at the system level. So far, two kinds of system have been investigated: first, systems that open when the relative humidity level increases (by changes to their surface porosity, these systems have the ability to autonomously ventilate once a defined level of relative humidity is reached),[10] and second, systems that operate in an inverse manner, reacting to a rise of relative humidity, for example through approaching rainfall, by closing the structure, thus providing weather-sensitive convertible surfaces. In addition, because relative humidity is temperature dependent, these systems also show a degree of relative thermal responsiveness: given a swift drop in temperature, the surfaces also close. Using functional prototypes, these surface behaviours have been investigated extensively, both as laboratory experiments in a climate chamber with carefully controlled humidity changes and in long-term tests set in the environment and exposed to the real humidity cycles of the central European climate.

System morphology plays an important role in the development of these locally controlled, responsive surface structures, as each region independently senses local humidity concentrations and changes the surface accordingly. The related microclimatic conditions across the surfaces, which are simultaneously affected by and do affect the system's behaviour, are directly influenced by both the local element geometry as well as the system morphology. Accounting for the complex reciprocity of individual element as well as overall system responsiveness and related macro- and microthermodynamic modulations, an integrative computational design process was developed as part of the research presented here in order to derive more specific system morphologies as compared to the relatively simple and regular geometry of the testing prototypes.[11] In this process, the surface geometry is algorithmically generated and controlled through a number of parameters and constraints based on the material's anatomy, characteristics and behaviour.

The evolution of the system morphology is based on iterative changes to the variables of the algorithmic processes and the evaluation of the generated results. This computational design process allows a relatively simple system consisting only of four-, five-, six- and seven-sided polygonal elements to specifically adapt its morphological features as, for example, local element density and overall curvature, in response to contextual requirements. In addition, this morphology enables the integration of the responsive and structural elements in one system. Through additional lamination with altering grain directionality, the reactive elements gain structural capacity towards the perimeter of each responsive component. In the overall system, this local thickening of the system results in a structural lattice with a responsive surface.

The responsive skin system has been long-term tested for half a year in the real humidity cycles of the central European climate. In constant exchange with the surrounding environment it shows consistent and reliable opening and closing cycles in response to changes in ambient relative humidity and temperature.

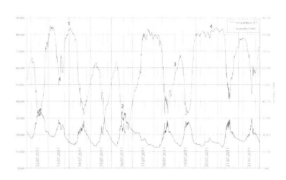

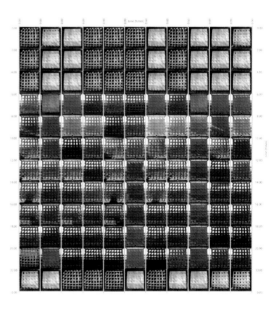

Fred Ernst, Maria Hänichen, Norbert Jundt, Florian Krampe, Georg Ladurner, Michael Pelzer, Michael Schnell, Christopher Voss and Steffen Reichert, Hygroscopic Envelope Prototype, Institute for Computational Design (ICD), University of Stuttgart, Stuttgart, 2010–11
top: A full-scale, functional responsive skin prototype shown in open (top) and closed state (bottom) demonstrates the material's capacity to be at the same time embedded sensor, no-energy motor and regulating element

Steffen Reichert and Achim Menges, Responsive Surface Structure II, Department for Form Generation and Materialisation, HFG Offenbach, Offenbach am Main, Germany, 2008
bottom: A responsive system component was developed that can adapt its shape by being based on either a four-, five-, six- or seven-sided polygon. In addition, the component does not require a substructure; the responsive tip is an extension of the thicker structural frame.

Climactive Architecture: Ecological Embedding

Perceiving wood's innate environmental responsiveness as a versatile behavioural characteristic rather than a difficult to control deficiency allows for teasing out a new performative capacity from one of the oldest and most common construction materials at our disposal. In architecture, this provides an interesting alternative for thinking about responsiveness not as something that is superimposed on inert material constructs by means of high-tech equipment, but rather as a no-tech capacity already fully embedded in the material itself.

The ramifications of releasing this material capacity by employing the aforementioned research in an architectural context may be profound, as the work on the FAZ Summer Pavilion (2010) begins to indicate. Situated on the northern embankment of the River Main in Frankfurt's city centre, the pavilion provides an interior extension of this popular public space. Based on the integral structural and hygroscopic responsive system introduced above, the entire envelope of the summer pavilion reacts to weather changes. On sunny or dry days with relatively low ambient humidity, the surface is fully opened. When the weather changes and rainfall approaches, the related increase in relative ambient humidity automatically triggers an autonomous response and the structure closes to form a weatherproof skin. Once the rain is over, the relative humidity level drops again, causing the pavilion to open. Similarly, the envelope closes at night with considerably lower temperatures than during the day, and reopens with the rise of temperature in the morning.

Beyond fulfilling merely the functional requirements of a convertible building skin, the autonomous, passive actuation of the FAZ pavilion's surface provides for a unique convergence of environmental and spatial experience. The perception of the delicate, locally varied and ever-changing environmental dynamics is intensified through the subtle and silent movement of the responsive envelope. The changing surface literally embodies the capacity to sense, actuate and regulate, all within the material itself. This suggests the possibility of a strikingly simple yet truly ecologically embedded architecture that is in constant feedback and interaction with its environment. ⌂

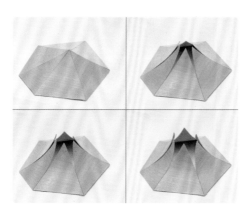

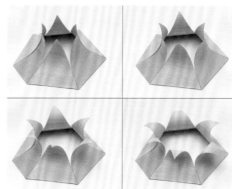

Steffen Reichert and Achim Menges,
Responsive Surface Structure II,
Department for Form Generation
and Materialisation, HFG Offenbach,
Offenbach am Main, Germany, 2008
below: Through an evolutionary
computational design process a
relatively simple system consisting
only of four-, five-, six- and seven-
sided polygonal elements can
specifically adapt its morphological
features such as, for example,
local element density and overall
curvature, to structural and contextual
requirements.

Notes

1. Alexander G Volkov, Tejumade Adesina, Vladislav S Markin and Emil Jovanov, 'Kinetics and Mechanism of Dionaea Muscipula Trap Closing', *Journal of Plant Physiology*, Vol 146 (2), 2008, pp 694–702.

2. Achim Menges, 'Material Performance – Responsive Surface Structures: Instrumentalising Moisture-Content Activated Dimensional Changes of Timber Components', in Δ *Versatility and Vicissitude in Morpho-Ecological Design*, Vol 78, No 2, 2008, pp 39–41.

3. Colin Dawson, Julian FV Vincent and Anne-Marie Rocca, 'How Pine Cones Open', *Nature*, Vol 390 18/25, December 1997, p 668.

4. E Reyssat and L Mahadevan, 'Hygromorphs: From Pine Cones to Biomimetic Bilayers', *Journal of the Royal Society Interface* 6, 2009, pp 951–7.

5. ID Cave, 'Wood Substance as a Water-Reactive Fibre Reinforced Composite', *Journal of Microscopy*, Vol 104 (1), 1975, pp 57–62.

6. John R Barnett and George Jeronimidis (eds), *Wood Quality and its Biological Basis,* Blackwell CRC Press (Oxford), 2003.

7. John M Dinwoodie, *Timber: Its Nature and Behaviour*, E&F Spon Press (London), 2000.

8. Rudi Wagenführ, *Anatomie des Holzes*, Drw Verlag (Leinfelden-Echterdingen), 1999.

9. Christen Skaar, *Wood-Water Relations*, Springer-Verlag (Berlin), 1988.

10. Achim Menges, 'Performative Wood: Integral Computational Design for Timber Construction', in *Reform: Building a Better Tomorrow, Proceedings of the 29th Conference of the Association For Computer Aided Design In Architecture (ACADIA)*, Chicago, 21–25 October 2009, pp 66–74.

11. Steffen Reichert and Achim Menges, 'Responsive Surface Structures', *Bionik: Patente aus der Natur, Proceedings of Fifth Bionics Conference*, Bionik-Innovations-Centrum (B-I-C), Bremen, 22–23 October 2010, pp 28–35.

Achim Menges, Steffen Reichert and
Scheffler+Partner, FAZ Pavilion, Frankfurt,
2010
below: The envelope of the pavilion is
designed as an integral structural and
climate-responsive material system
providing for a novel convergence of
environmental and spatial experiences. As
the responsive capacity is embedded in
the material itself, no additional technical
equipment or supply of energy is required.
When the weather changes from sun (top)
to rainfall (bottom), the related increase
in relative ambient humidity automatically
triggers an autonomous response and the
structure closes to form a weatherproof skin.

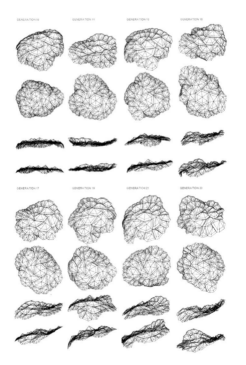

Sean Ahlquist and Achim Menges

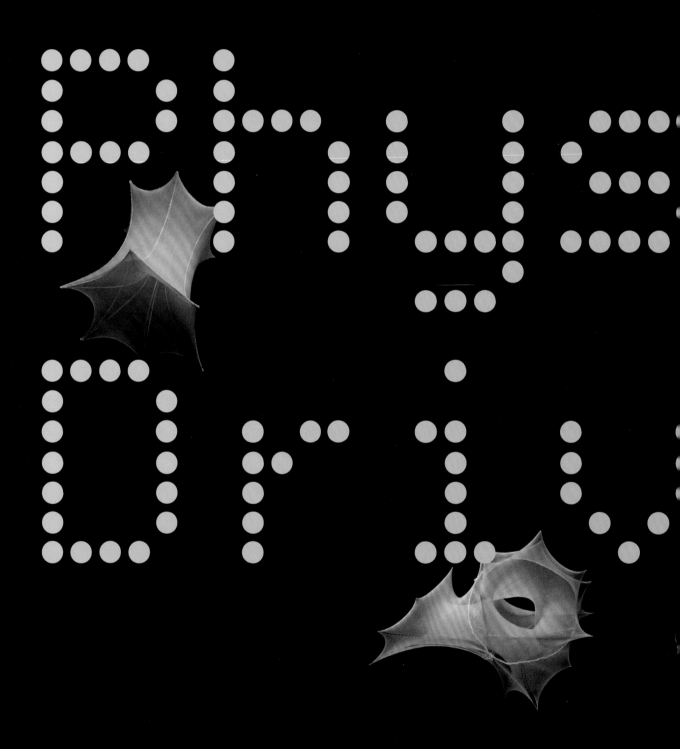

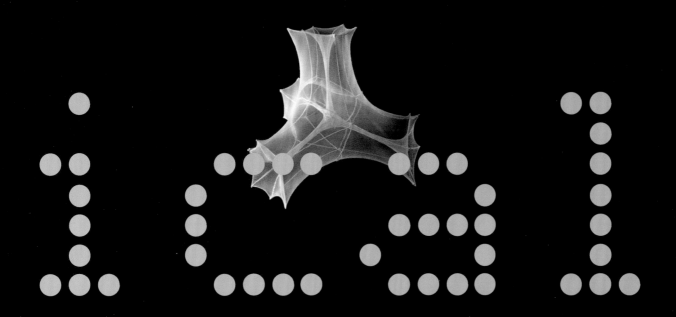

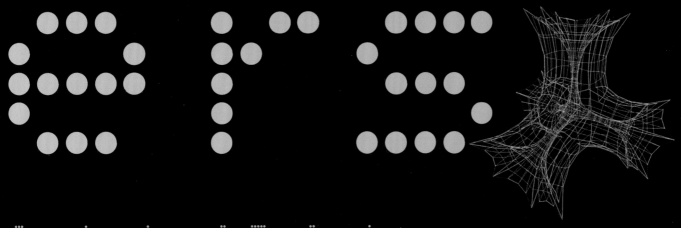

ideal

Synthesis of Evolutionary Developments and Force-Driven Design ■

Primarily admired as feats of engineering, tension-driven material systems are notoriously difficult for architects to employ. Though the shape and structural capacity of these systems are defined by the imposition of force, they do not follow predictable geometric or mathematical patterns. In this article, **Sean Ahlquist and Achim Menges** present their research into force-driven material systems, and explain the development of an architectural design framework that allows for these complex material interdependencies to be not only resolved, but also explored as multiple possible equilibrium states. ■

There is a rich history in the founding of design processes that, in simultaneity, resolve form, the structuring of form, and the formation of form. Such processes exist in the well-documented examples from Gaudí's hanging chain models for the Sagrada Família (1883–) in Barcelona to Frei Otto's more recent experiments in physical form-finding with soap bubbles, woven textiles and fixed node meshes. In these instances it is easiest to simply refer to form not as the result, but as the collection of processes related to generation, materialisation and physicality in operation: the morphology or, ultimately, the gestalt. What is of particular relevance in constructing novel approaches to the development of integrated architectural systems is the eschewing of representation and primacy of geometry for engaging the simulation of system- and context-intrinsic affecters for explorative means. The systems of generation and the systems of operation are intimately aligned, not representatively layered.[1]

What these precedents address is the complexity in resolving interdependencies and, specifically, those that range the scale and hierarchies of the system at hand. The most primary affecter and effecter is matter, and not material, as that is possibly too concrete for a described arrangement. As matter, fundamental principles, both physical and atmospheric, can be expressed to, in process, develop morphologically varied material organisations. Otto's soap-film studies are the perfect example of this; the arrangement of matter in a completely equalised state of force distribution

Boyan Mihaylov and Viktoriya Nikolova, Hyper-Toroidal Deep Surface Studies, Institute for Computational Design (ICD), University of Stuttgart, Stuttgart, 2011
below: Integrated tensioned surface and mesh morphologies based upon multiple hyper-toroidal cellular topologies derived through a computational design framework by Sean Ahlquist.

previous spread: Development of complexities in topology and panel description for individual cells through physical and computational experiments.

Sean Ahlquist, Behaviour-Based Modelling Environment, Institute for Computational Design (ICD), University of Stuttgart, Stuttgart, ongoing
Developed in the Java-based programming environment Processing, and utilising a particle system engine for form-finding, the environment exposes variables in topology, force description and material characterisation related to integrated tensioned mesh and surfaces systems. As a form of simulation, the environment serves to experiment with basic principles in tension-active systems and evolve complex yet feasible material morphologies.

Sean Ahlquist, Comparison in Calculating Behaviour, Institute for Computational Design (ICD), University of Stuttgart, Stuttgart, 2010
Comparison in calculating behaviour. Analysis in comparing methods, force description and geometric results between spring-based form-finding and simulation utilising Formfinder and MPanel, both finite element (FE) based solvers.

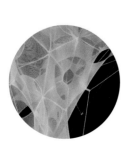

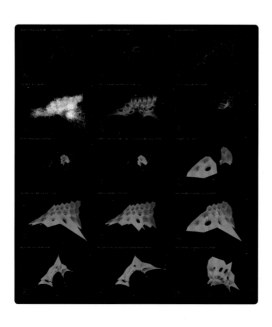

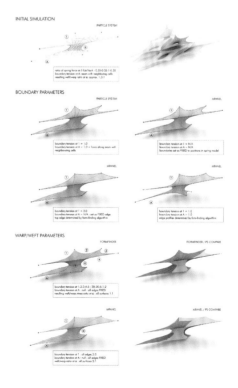

describes a surface whereby the particles within that surface space are in constant motion because of this equalisation.[2] Discovering material intelligence is at the core of resolving form complexity.

The term form-finding is often applied to such efforts in generating form through material organisation under the influence of internal and external pressures. There is a different nature between physical form-finding, which is the simulation of a specific circumstance of elements and forces, and computational form-finding, which is the iterative exploration of variable circumstances. Where material becomes introduced as a parameter of form-generation, it is often a representative measure based upon geometric rules in computation. In geometry only, interaction between material elements is not always solvable; the exacerbation of change from one element to the whole system (and back) cannot be captured within geometric relations or singular mathematical descriptions. What becomes constraint in computational form-finding is the qualification of matter and specification of behaviours by which matter of different types interact. Where materialisation in a representative model is autonomous, when formation is via the behaviour of matter, it is necessarily embedded and influencing.

These concepts are expressed in research related to the development of computational processes and novel morphologies for tension-defined surface and mesh systems (often referred to as tension-active membrane and cable-net structures). Addressing the physicality of the system in form and operation through computational processes is critical as their description cannot be stated mathematically. Only iterative processes which work to simulate the tension-force distribution generating surface position and structural rigidity are viable. The interdependencies of force and matter across scales and hierarchies compel a unique understanding, approach and framework to be devised, one that places behaviour over representation. The main question is how, as a process, the principles of behaviour are formed as transitional functions, executed to realise capacities in global behaviour, and translated to specify in fabrication and operation.

Where material becomes introduced as a parameter of form-generation, it is often a representative measure based upon geometric rules in computation.

Sean Ahlquist, Material Translation Algorithm, Institute for Computational Design (ICD), University of Stuttgart, Stuttgart, 2010
The algorithm translates the spring-force simulation data from Processing to cut templates for fabrication. The force and material elasticity are simultaneously calculated to allow for large panels to accomplish varying degrees of double curvature. The limits of double curvature are analysed in the geometry to define panel boundaries.

The complex topological form concept is generated through the association of multiple cylindrical mesh networks. The mapping of force is differentiated to articulate the resulting form, and unitised for materialisation and pre-stressing. Translation from computational force diagram to material is processed through digital material testing. Topology is mapped via the logic defined computationally, as interconnected cylindrical mesh networks.

Comparison between the computational model and physical prototype.

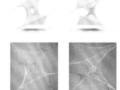

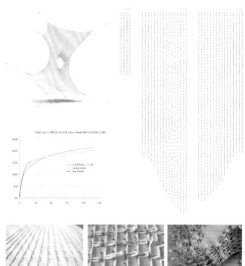

System Formation

As mentioned, form is not a static entity; rather, it serves as a system itself that embodies the interacting systems by which it was formed and how it operates. The statement a 'system of systems' should be expected, and not unfamiliar, but it is most critical in this instance to understand how the finality of the system is dealt with.[3] From a generative computational process forming architectural material systems, the finality can be understood as a homeostatic 'state' born of a 'state space'. The state space is not the collection of various results; it houses the functions that define the transitions from one state to another.[4] There is very minimal input in the manner of discrete descriptions within the state space. As such, the transitions consider previous events, subsequent events and neighbouring transitions, serving as a fundamental definition for behaviour in local events and homeostatic performance.[5]

Transition and behaviour serve as pivotal concepts in working with tension-active systems. Such systems are categorised by three basic types: saddle, cone and ridge-valley.[6] While all tension-active geometries can be broken down into these form concepts, it is the hybridisation between them that makes for an exhaustive set of possibilities in performance. The transition function at this level is in negotiating the logics of force, curvature and boundary condition as they characterise the different form concepts. The functions are not geometric, but rather the medium of force is activated within the state space to alter, affect and resolve the global solution. It is vital to recognise the generating aspect of the computational formation process as an informational generator whereby intelligence and specificity is only gained during and after the imposition of particular characteristics of matter (material and force).

In terms of computing the nature of tension-active systems, the initial precedent was set with Otto's process of developing highly material-specified scale models to which only hand calculations were necessary to augment the validation of the design. This was translated most directly into finite element analysis (FEA) via methods such as dynamic relaxation, force density and modified stiffness, where a simulation model tested the dynamics of tension loading on particular material and boundary parameters (pre-stressing) against additional external loading.[7]

Of course, what is apparent in these process examples is the need for completeness of the information prior to the activation of the process. In exploring the operational system, the process cannot be a matter of informational verification or informational organisation; it has to follow the logic by which the system forms in cumulative steps of negotiated principles of behaviour in the various forms of matter that make up the system.

Embedded Behaviour

Topology is a pivotal expression of cross-hierarchical behaviours. An overall topology may, in concept, depict the

---

Valentin Brenner and Sonya Templin, Cellular Deep Surface, Institute for Computational Design (ICD), University of Stuttgart, Stuttgart, 2010
Cylindrical cells are integrally tensioned, with some stiffened as composites to define a rigid boundary. Orientation is calibrated to consider surface exposure for use as an energy harvesting device.

Sean Ahlquist, Large-Scale Deep Surface, Institute for Computational Design (ICD), University of Stuttgart, Stuttgart, 2011
below and right: Study of the large-scale implementation of a deep surface system. Diagrid tensioned cable mesh spans approximately 10 metres (33 feet) while the depth of the tensioned surface cells ranges from 50 centimetres (20 inches) to 500 centimetres (197 inches). The inner ellipsoidal volume of the tensioned mesh is generated through the interaction of the meshes and tensioned surface membranes. A prototype was developed during the SmartGeometry 2010 Workshop with cluster co-leader Achim Menges and participating students.

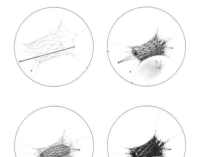

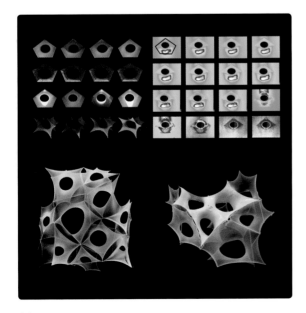

global 'shape', as much as this may align with the form concepts of a plane as saddle, a cylinder as cone, or extend to more complex toroidal or hyper-toroidal networks. Most significant, though, is the use of topology as the medium by which force is expressed. The network of elements explicitly describes the pathways of force. However, there are subtle distinctions that equate a certain understanding of material behaviour. In a tensioned surface (textile or foil), force will look to equalise across an entire bounded area. This can be accounted in the materialisation of a textile as a series of woven fibres. In a tensioned mesh (cable or otherwise linear material element) where the intersections are fixed, force is resolved only locally at each node.[8] Force will search for equilibrium, but that equilibrium does not have to be equalised. As topology can be constructed via differentiated local definitions, it may be that the overall network has some concept of shape, but that the local behaviour can easily vary between that of a distributed-force surface or localised-force mesh.

As topology can be constructed via differentiated local definitions, it may be that the overall network has some concept of shape, but that the local behaviour can easily vary between that of a distributed-force surface or localised-force mesh.

Where topology realises form is in its activation as a particle system. Particle systems are computational physics-based engines that simulate primary forces such as gravity, tension, compression, drag, magnetism and pressure. The use of springs, based upon the principle of Hooke's law of elasticity,[9] to affect topology in determining force equilibrium and form serves as a thorough informational system for exploring complex tensioned morphologies. While particle systems have been explored in computational design, they are often not engaged to provide information beyond the position after a certain equilibrium state has been realised. The information that distinguishes moments of surface or mesh and the characteristics of distributed force, equally or unequally, are all pivotal in accomplishing a generating system that recognises the interdependencies of structure and materialisation of the operational system.

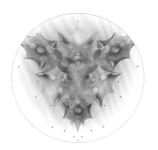

Boyan Mihaylov and Viktoriya Nikolova, Hyper-Toroidal Deep Surface Studies, Institute for Computational Design (ICD), University of Stuttgart, Stuttgart, 2011
left and below: Comparison between the computational model and physical prototype. The translational algorithm is calibrated with the textile performance, allowing for the physical prototype, while geometrically and topologically complex, to be aligned with the computational model.

Physical prototype at the approximate size of 120 x 80 x 150 centimetres (47 x 31 x 59 inches).

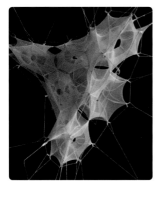

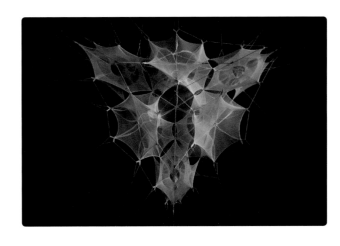

Integral Translation

Distinguished from FEA, the parameters and feedback from a particle system are relative and translational. While strength is a spring variable, it does not equate literally to material stiffness. The output from a spring, its force, is relative to the entire network, but not at a particular scale until it has been qualified with specific material properties. This is, in fact, a limitation of most particle systems, as conventionally the solvers do not function efficiently when programmed to solve for relatively inelastic elements. Yet through calibrating the principles of material elasticity and the properties of input and output from a particle system, it has been found that materialisation can be both extracted informationally and embedded parametrically.

What must ultimately be solved in tension-active systems is the panellisation of the system. While current design technologies have made the automation of transferring geometric form to fabrication data ubiquitous, it is often not embedded in the parameterisation as influential for forming the structural logic. This is mission-critical for exploring advanced capacities in form for tension-defined systems. Another layering of negotiation across scales of the system is the relation between double curvature, degree and distribution of force and material elasticity. As the system materialised is pre-stressed, the material components have to be translated into their unstressed state for manufacturing to then result in the desired geometry when assembled and stressed.

> *What must ultimately be solved in tension–active systems is the panellisation of the system. While current design technologies have made the automation of transferring geometric form to fabrication data ubiquitous, it is often not embedded in the parameterisation as influential for forming the structural logic.*

Michael Pelzer and Christine Rosemann,
Perforated Deep Surface Prototype,
Institute for Computational Design (ICD),
University of Stuttgart, Stuttgart, 2011
Physical prototype at the approximate size
of 120 x 80 x 150 centimetres (47 x 31 x
59 inches).

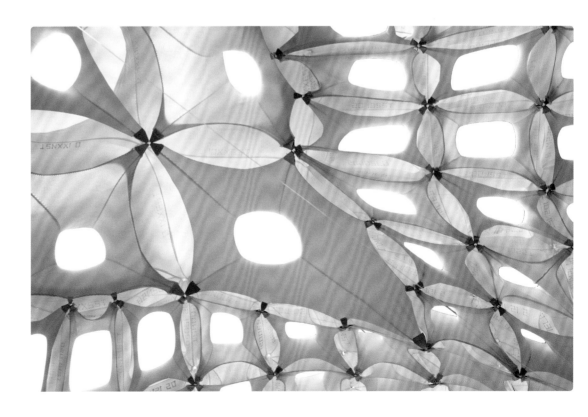

Evolving Morphospaces

As the generating system is a compilation of various processes, the processes cannot be explored thoroughly or controlled through a single generation, analysis and feedback step. The best way to organise this framework is in the evolution of 'morphospaces'. A developmental morphospace is defined by the body of variables that encapsulate a particular ontogenetic process while compared against evolutionary pressures.[10] In this case, a morphospace may define the topological description of shape. The development of a particular form out of that morphospace will subsequently produce a new morphospace based on the parameterisation of variable panel descriptions measured against criteria related to material properties.

Within this framework lies the possibility for developing impressive and viable complexities for tension-active material systems. Such complexities, in the research shown here, have concentrated on and explored geometric capacities in materially differentiated (surface and mesh) morphologies. Given that force, as stated, is the primary medium, the significant challenge in instrumentalising such systems is the control over the possibilities in formal descriptions. As this establishes a new morphospace, additional capacities in spatial and atmospheric modulation can be pursued. ⌂

Notes

1. Christopher Alexander argues the distinctions between discerning the behaviour of a system and instrumentalising it within a generating system. One functions as a view of an operational 'whole' while the other deciphers the integrated systems functioning as unique parts. C Alexander, 'Systems Generating Systems', *D*, No 7/6, December 2003, pp 90–1.
2. Manuel DeLanda, *Intensive Science & Virtual Philosophy*, Continuum (New York), 2002, p 15.
3. Ludwig von Bertalanffy states this as 'equifinality', one aspect of which is that a system is in constant fluctuation between states balanced through the impetus of feedback. L von Bertalanffy, *General System Theory: Foundations, Development, Applications*, George Braziller (New York), 1969, p 46.
4. J Holland, *Emergence: From Chaos to Order*, Oxford University Press (Oxford), 1998, p 132–3.
5. Referring to the work of JS Gero and his framework for function-behaviour-structure, behaviour serves to inform and specify symbolic or schematised knowledge. A Goel, *Structure, Behavior and Function of Complex Systems: The SBF Modeling Language*, Georgia University of Technology (Atlanta, GA), 2009, p 7.
6. M Bechthold, *Innovative Surface Structures: Technologies and Applications*, Taylor & Francis (Abingdon, Oxfordshire), 2008, p 48.
7. E Moncrieff, 'Systems for Lightweight Structure Design: the State-of-the-Art and Current Developments', in Eugenio Oñate and Bernd Kröplin (eds), *Textile Composites and Inflatable Structures*, Springer (Dordrecht), 2005, p 19.
8. WJ Lewis, *Tension Structures: Form and Behaviour*, Thomas Telford (London), 2003, pp 12–15.
9. Hooke's law of elasticity states that a force can be measured from the degree of displacement of a spring from its equilibrium state multiplied by a spring constant: $F=-K*(rL-L)$. This provides an efficient calculation of force, but does not recognise non-linear behaviour if K is a constant. See JE Gordon, *The New Science of Strong Materials or Why You Don't Fall Through the Floor*, Princeton University Press (Princeton, NJ), rev edn, 2006, p 36.
10. GJ Eble, 'Developmental and Non-Developmental Morphospaces in Evolutionary Biology', Santa Fe Institute (Santa Fe, NM), p 4.

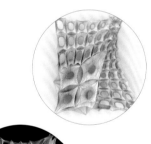
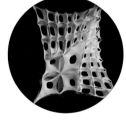

Comparison between the computational model and physical prototype.

Strategy for individual cells describing a continuous surface with variable cylindrical apertures. The tensioned mesh and anchoring location serve to contort the overall geometry. Variation in the warp-and-weft force description defines differences in aperture dimensions. Acoustic modulation is considered when varying aperture diameter, depth and wall thickness.

Skylar Tibbits, Logic Matter,
Massachusetts Institute of Technology
(MIT), Cambridge, Massachusetts, 2010
The sphere volume shown is described
by a non-intersecting random path tour
around the exterior surface. This single path
along the surface describes a sequence of
rotational angles to approximate the exterior
of the sphere's geometry.

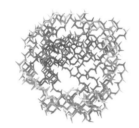

DESIGN TO SELF-ASSEMBLY

The increasing power of design software, the
widespread availability of digital fabrication and
growing complexity of our built environment are
in stark contrast to the inefficient techniques that
currently plague the construction industry. Today's
processes of assembly can be fundamentally reimagined by looking at biological systems that
are building structures with far more complexity,
information capacity and assembly instructions
than even the most advanced structures possible
with current technologies. **Skylar Tibbits** explains
that the key ingredient embedded within these
natural systems is self-assembly. He outlines
four principles for designing systems that build
themselves, and shows a number of projects that
demonstrate first steps towards this new mode of
architectural production.

By all measures our society is increasing in complexity, whether it is our expanding population, our reliance on digital technologies or the extremely large/small/precise/complex structures we aim to build with new tools and processes. Similarly, the design and construction of our physical world is stuck in an endless battle of increasing design capabilities with outdated construction techniques, brought on by breakthroughs in design tools and the expediency of digital fabrication. These exciting tools for design and fabrication are quickly leaping bounds above our capabilities for assembly and construction.

Proposed here is an alternative vision for the future of construction, one that scales from the most minute of biological structures to the largest of infrastructures. This assembly system reimagines what we have learned from the Industrial Revolution by slamming together the digital and physical worlds. Rather than taking raw materials, sending them through a machine or process that is inherently fighting tolerances, errors and energy consumption to arrive at a desired product, we should be directly embedding assembly information into raw materials, then watching as the materials assemble themselves. This process is self-assembly and it is the future of construction.

Nearly every biological process, from our body's proteins and DNA to cell replication and regeneration, utilises self-assembly for construction. These biological structures are far more complex, intricate and precise than any human-built structure to grace the earth. Further, they are capable of self-repair for longevity, self-replication for reproduction, and growing or mutating new structures. If we are going to build structures more adaptable to the current demands of our society and environment, our construction techniques will need to keep up with the rapid developments in design and fabrication, and we will therefore need to find smarter systems of assembly. These new possibilities of assembly must rely on smarter parts, not more complex machines. This is self-assembly where our parts build themselves and we design with forces, material properties and states, where construction looks more like computer science or biology rather than sledgehammers and welders. In order to design with this new future of self-assembly, we need only four simple ingredients: 1) simple assembly sequences; 2) programmable parts; 3) force or energy of activation; and 4) error correction and redundancy.

Simple Assembly Sequences

The first ingredient needed for designing physical systems of self-assembly is a simple sequence of instructions. This is the DNA sequence for what we want to build. Rather than the A,C,T and G of our DNA, we can use building instructions, on/off, left/right/up/down etc. This instruction set should remain as simple as possible because, as you can imagine, if you have a simple step-by-step instruction sequence to build a wall it would be far easier than following a recursive or fractal definition, though the latter may provide possibilities for compressing more complex structures into fewer steps. Essentially, we need algorithmic descriptions to construct any desired 3-D structure. Luckily, through algorithms like Hamiltonian paths and Euler tours (various ways to draw

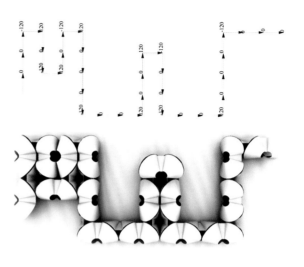

Skylar Tibbits, Decibot, Massachusetts Institute of Technology (MIT), Cambridge, Massachusetts, 2009
below: Single sequence of rotational angles representing the 2-D letters 'MIT' and a rendered depiction of the resultant folded robotic chain.

Skylar Tibbits, voltaDom, Massachusetts Institute of Technology (MIT), Cambridge, Massachusetts, 2011
below: The voltaDom is made up of 1.2 x 2.4 metre (4 x 8 foot) sheets of powder-coated white aluminium and white polyethylene plastic cut on a 1.5 x 3 metre (5 x 10 foot) three-axis CNC router. Thousands of parts were assembled on site, each containing nomenclature, bolt and rivet holes.

bottom: The voltaDom installation was designed and built for MIT's 150th anniversary celebration and FAST festival. It represents a new type of experimental structure and installation generated by computer code and made possible by new technologies in digital fabrication.

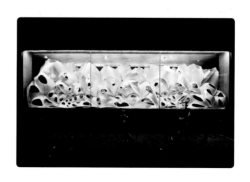

a single line through an arbitrary set of points), it has been demonstrated that any given 1-D, 2-D or 3-D geometry can be described by a single sequence or folded line.[1]

The Macrobot and Decibot are large-scale reconfigurable robot chains that take in a single sequence of fold angles and can change shape on demand, from any 1-D to 2-D or 3-D shape. The assembly instructions might look like [−120, 0, 0, 120, 0, 0...], or a series of joint angles that are passed down a robotic chain. Each robotic unit reads the instructions, takes out the angle at its specified location, rotates to the corresponding angle (until a sensor indicates it has reached the desired placement), and then passes the instruction sequence down the chain. This happens for all of the units (and could happen for any number of units or in any sequence) in order to fold from one 3-D shape into another.

Programmable Parts

The second ingredient for self-assembly is programmable parts, or smart joints. Just as DNA has base pairs, or proteins have discrete amino acids with unique shapes, attractions and rotation angles, we need to design systems with simple yet smartly discrete (and finite) elements.[2] These parts should be able to have at least two states and should correspond to the instruction sequences; for example, on/off or left/right/up/down etc. When we create an aggregation or sequence of these parts, interconnected with one another, every joint should be able to freely switch between states depending on each step in the instructions. This means we are looking to build structures from simple switches; each switch can be activated to change from one state to another depending on its placement or relationship to an external condition.

Neil Gershenfeld of the Center for Bits and Atoms at the Massachusetts Institute of Technology (MIT) explains how a system of truly programmable parts could actually carry their own assembly instructions: '[the] medium is quite literally its message, internally carrying instructions on its own assembly. Such programmable materials are remote from modern manufacturing practice, but they are all around us.'[3] Demonstrating this programmability, a series of building blocks called Logic Matter embed digital logic into a simple geometric mechanism.[4] The tetrahedron-based geometry is assembled by the user, piece by piece, only allowing the placement of the correct computation based on the previous move and a newly input unit.

Logic Matter demonstrates a unit with programmability, including two input faces and two output faces that combine together to define a new state. This building block goes even further than a simple binary switch by embedding digital logic, the fundamental element of computation. In this module, digital logic is embedded through a digital NAND (Not-And) Logic Gate, through a simple geometric mechanism. This means that the instructions for assembly are built directly into the materials as a primitive hard drive and processor, the units working hand-in-hand with the user to store assembly information, build and compute on next moves, check previous moves and assemble digital-discrete structures in 3-D. Logic Matter can take in a simple sequence of assembly instructions and inform the user to act upon them, or actually generate its own sequence of instructions for the next build.

Skylar Tibbits, Decibot, Massachusetts Institute of Technology (MIT), Cambridge, Massachusetts, 2009
above: The Decibot is a full-scale reconfigurable robotic chain developed to demonstrate self-assembly and programmable matter.

below (left and right): Image series showing the Decibot, a large-scale reconfigurable robotic chain, folding from a 1-D to a 3-D geometry.

Force of Activation

The next ingredient for self-assembly is the force or energy required to get a structure from point A to point B. This is the muscles of the system, or the energy input to make the smart joints act on each of the instructions that are sent. Biologically, this comes from polarity or hydroscopic and hydrophilic properties to name just a few. Robotically, the force of activation is usually electricity supplied to a motor and gear system. However, if we want to focus on architectural-scale structures we will ultimately need large forces and many parts (thousands or millions) at macroscale lengths, thus demanding we pay attention to passive energy sources. (Additionally, our industries should ultimately be moving towards sustainable and energy-producing, rather than energy-consuming, systems.) Passively, our design for self-assembly can utilise a variety of energy sources: heat and expansion/contraction of materials, fluids and capillary action or hydraulics, pneumatics, gravity, wind resistance, shaking, pre- and post-tension or compression members, springs and a plethora of other opportunities.

The Biased Chains prototype demonstrates a completely passive system that is capable of folding from 1-D to 3-D structures, with only one programmable part connected in alternating orientations, simply through the act of shaking. In this example, the user assembles a 1-D chain of elements. At each step, the orientation of the part dictates the fold angle and thus becomes the simple sequence of instructions for building any rigid 3-D structure. Once the sequence of units is assembled, the user simply shakes the chain, adding stochastic movement and energy that automatically switches each of the units into the correct orientation to successfully build rigid structures. Biased Chains is a great example of a completely scaleable system, utilising passive energy, simple instruction sequences and programmable parts, effectively letting the materials build themselves.

Error Correction

The final ingredient for self-assembly is error correction and redundancy to ensure that we build accurate structures that are not prone to constant failure. One of the best examples to utilise error correction lies at the turning point from the analogue to digital communication industries. Shannon and Von Neumann's introduction of digital logic in the 1940s gave us the ability to send information across unreliable signals and guarantee reliable communication.[5] Gershenfeld explains that we can easily send and receive 10^{23} bits of information and our bodies can be made from 10^{23} atoms, but asks why we cannot come close to making physical structures with 10^{23} parts.[6]

Digital communication relies on systems of majority voting and sending far more information than necessary to guarantee accurate communication.[7] Similarly, many biological systems have methods of error checking with redundant information, a proofreading mechanism, error correction, and a system that discards failed attempts.[8] In the case of building physical self-assembly structures, this means that we need to build with redundancy or interconnectedness. Single points of connection will be prone to structural failures or assembly errors and thus we need to add additional connections that continually tie back.

Skylar Tibbits, Macrobot, Massachusetts Institute of Technology (MIT), Cambridge, Massachusetts, 2009
above: Sequence of images showing the Macrobot system folding from a 1-D chain into a 2-D and 3-D geometry then back into a 1-D chain.

Skylar Tibbits, Passive Folder, Massachusetts Institute of Technology (MIT), Cambridge, Massachusetts, 2010
below: The Passive Folder is a programmable linear chain that demonstrates a three-state mechanism with rotational angles at 0, 120 and –120.

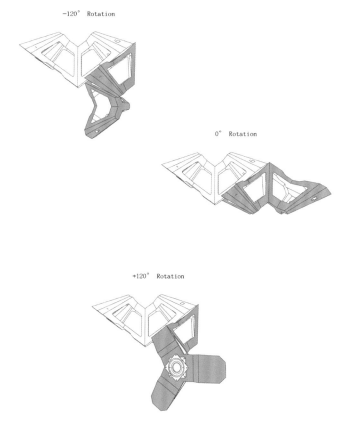

−120° Rotation

0° Rotation

+120° Rotation

Skylar Tibbits, Logic Matter,
Massachusetts Institute of Technology
(MIT), Cambridge, Massachusetts, 2010
top: Diagram showing a primitive
tetrahedron unit with input and output
faces, resulting in a NAND (Not-And)
Logic Gate and spatial computation when
the user assembles the units.

centre and bottom: Two possible simple
assemblies of Logic Matter: the input of
[1,1] results in the computation [0] or the
input of a unit DOWN (top), and the input
of [0,0] results in the computation [1] or
the input of a unit UP (bottom).

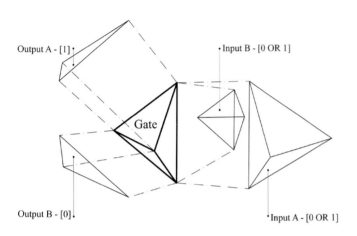

Output A - [1]

Input B - [0 OR 1]

Gate

Output B - [0]

Input A - [0 OR 1]

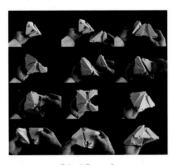

$$[1,1] = 0$$

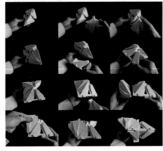

$$[0,0] = 1$$

Within Logic Matter, each unit takes two inputs: one from the previous unit that it is attached to (the last unit placed); and the other from the placement of a new unit by the user. Thus, the unit looks to the previous move plus the user's latest input and performs logic computation to allow the placement of a new unit only in the properly computed position. After each computation, there is only one output. This means that for every two inputs we only continue to grow from one output, thus there is always a unit of redundancy. As the system grows and begins to turn up/down/left/right, these redundant units interconnect with one another forming strong structural connections and tie-backs. This redundant information also contains one of the inputs as a physical history, or blueprint, of the built structure. In order to allow systems to self-replicate, these redundant units are the key ingredient to reading the assembly instructions directly from the material, requiring no additional information to build an exact replica.

The Future
The future of our physical world is dependent upon our developments in fabrication and construction, inevitably requiring smarter materials and more intelligent processes of assembly. Ultimately, we will need to build structures bigger, smaller, more precise or with less energy than humanly possible today. This directly points to the inevitable revolution that is before us, one where our structures build themselves, can compute and adapt on demand, and where assembly looks more like biological processes than construction sites. We must be able to embed information into materials and have smarter parts, not just smarter machines.

If we utilise self-assembly as the next design and construction tool in our digital tool belts, then we may be able to solve some of the world's most urgent problems of adaptability, deployability and efficiency. From earthquake-resistant structures with programmable joints between beams and columns, activated by the shaking of the ground to become flexible or rigid on demand, or quickly deployable disaster-relief structures dropped from helicopters that utilise wind resistance and gravity to unfold fully erected and inhabitable, these large-scale problems can be tackled by designing around discrete parts and simple forces that translate elements from point A to point B. Self-assembly urges the design and building industries to rethink their processes of making, to look back at what we have learned from digital information, biology and mechanical computers, and take charge of the powers that are at (or literally within) our fingertips. Self-assembly is the inevitable revolution that faces our physical world. ◮

Notes

1. Jonathan Bachrach, V Zykov and S Griffith, *Folding Arbitrary 3D Shapes with Space-Filling Chain Robots: Folded Configuration Design as 3D Hamiltonian Path through Target Solid*, Makani Power (Alameda, CA) 2009. See also Erik Demaine and Joseph O'Rourke, *Geometric Folding Algorithms: Linkages, Origami, Polyhedra*, Cambridge University Press (Cambridge), 2007.

2. George A Popescu, 'Digital Materials for Digital Fabrication', Master of Science Thesis, Massachusetts Institute of Technology (MIT), 2007.

3. Neil Gershenfeld, *FAB: The Coming Revolution on your Desktop – From Personal Computers to Personal Fabrication*, Basic Books (New York), 2005, p 238.

4. Skylar Tibbits, 'Logic Matter: Digital Logic as Heuristics for Physical Self-Guided-Assembly', Master of Science Thesis, Massachusetts Institute of Technology (MIT), 2010.

5. Gershenfeld, op cit, p 235. See also John Von Neumann, *Theory of Self-Reproducing Automata*, University of Illinois Press (Urbana, IL and London), 1966.

6. Gershenfeld, op cit, p 240.

7. Ibid, p 235.

8. Ibid, p 240.

Skylar Tibbits, Biased Chains, Massachusetts Institute of Technology (MIT), Cambridge, Massachusetts, 2010
top: Biased Chains is a simple chain of connected parts, each containing a binary switch that the user activates by shaking the chain. Each part then switches into the programmed sequence and the chains fold from any 1-D geometry to any 3-D structure. It is a completely passive system capable of self-assembly through a simple shaking force.

bottom: Logic Matter is a system built upon redundant information. The white units are redundant information used as input for the growth of a structure. They provide structural redundancy and store assembly information like a hard drive. The grey units are the primary unit providing computation and the linear sequence of growth.

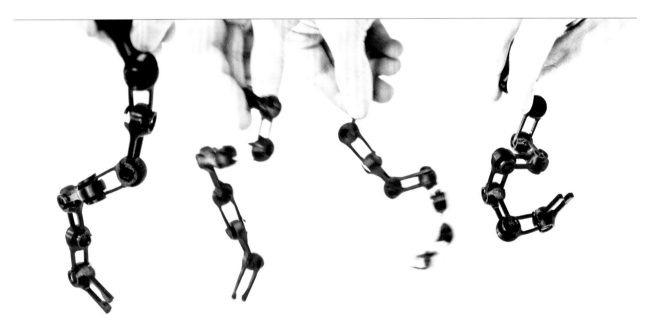

Self–assembly urges the design and building industries to rethink their processes of making, to look back at what we have learned from digital information, biology and mechanical computers, and take charge of the powers that are at (or literally within) our fingertips.

Karola Dierichs and Achim Menges

AGGRE
STRUC

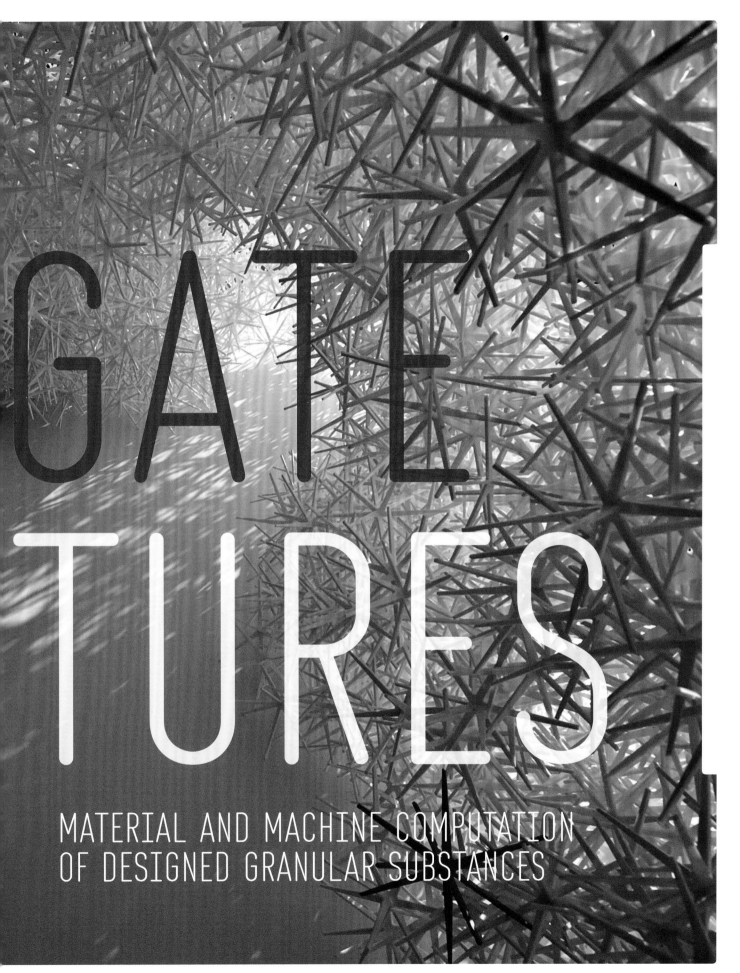

GATE TURES

MATERIAL AND MACHINE COMPUTATION
OF DESIGNED GRANULAR SUBSTANCES

In inanimate nature, large masses of granular substances are in constant processes of formation through perpetual cycles of erosion and accretion. What if architecture was to emulate this behaviour and allow for its own continuous reconfiguration? **Karola Dierichs and Achim Menges** establish the notion of an 'aggregate architecture'. Composed of large numbers of unbound yet designed granules, aggregates are based on a fundamentally different logic of construction. In contrast to assembly systems, aggregates materially compute their overall constructional configuration and shape as spatiotemporal behavioural patterns, with an equal ability for both: the stable character of a solid material and the rapid reconfigurability of a fluid.

Architecture is typically conceptualised as one of the most permanent and stable forms of human production. As a consequence it is commonly conceived as precisely planned, fully defined and ordered in stable assemblies of material elements. However, this conceptualisation only applies on a certain time scale. In the end, what appears to be stable and permanent are temporal configurations of elements exposed to various pressures for change. While the cyclic occurrence of these pressures seems to accelerate increasingly, in most architectural systems change can only happen by means of demolition and rebuilding.

Aggregates, that is, loose granular substances, offer a radically different model for both construction and constructional changes in architecture. Rather than conceiving of discrete phases of static configuration and interspersed reconfiguration as emblematic for assembly systems, aggregates suggest a perpetual mode of (re)construction, where stability is an intrinsic part of, rather than opposed to, destabilisation. This possibility arises because aggregates induce a fundamentally distinct principle of construction: as opposed to assembly systems, granulates as a material compute their overall structure and form through spatiotemporal patterns of behaviour. These configurations have the capacity to act both with the stability of a solid material on the one hand and the fast reconfigurability of a liquid on the other.

The research presented here investigates aggregate architectures as both an alternative intellectual model for design thinking and a pragmatic approach towards novel ways of construction. Thus it operates on three scalar axes: 1) in time, investigating the behavioural patterns of granular substances and

Karola Dierichs, Aggregate Architectures, Institute for Computational Design (ICD), University of Stuttgart, Stuttgart, 2011
previous spread: A system model of 50,000 industrially produced designed particles is poured and arranged to form interconnected aggregate vaults.

below (all): If critical particles or boundary conditions are adjusted, the granulate reconfigures from one stable state to the other.

the related strategic acceleration and deceleration of change and reconfiguration; 2) in space, exploring an increase of aggregate particle size from the small scale found in natural granular material towards larger designed and manufactured particles; and 3) in specificity, developing particle shapes not through an increase of differentiation by assigning particular functions to them as in elements for assembly systems, but rather by reducing the shape range to a few generic types that, in an accumulative manner, are capable of achieving functional gradation and variable performances across the overall system.

So what are aggregates? An example can be found in the infinite numbers of sand grains that gather to configure the material known to us as 'sand'. Sand formations move in cycles of erosion and accretion, and rather than becoming redundant or destroyed they merely reconfigure into continuously variant yet morphologically self-similar formations.[1] Substances like sand consist of large numbers of unbound, non-cohesive elements and are generally known as granular material or aggregates. In many ways granular materials do not resemble a single phase of matter, but display properties and behaviour similar to solids, liquids and even gases, though it is important to note that they also show properties unique to granular materials in each of these states. The granular material behaves like a solid if the grains are in a comparatively stable state, which means the level of each grain particle's energy is low and the grains are rather stationary relative to each other. However, if the grains lose contact with each other through the induction of energy, for example by pouring or shaking, the granular material fluidises and changes to a liquid-like state showing behaviour similar to non-Newtonian liquids. In this way granular materials combine a liquid's amorphous character and inherent ability for change and reconfiguration with the stability and structural capacity of solids.[2]

Aggregate Architecture

The architectural implications of these material characteristics have been rarely explored yet suggest a wide range of interesting possibilities. In an 'aggregate architecture' the specificity of the architectural system does not result from a designed plan and its precisely defined constituent parts, but solely through the characteristics of the individual elements and their cumulative behaviour. Understanding of these systems cannot be gained through deliberate planning, only through observation of their behaviour and the collection of cumulative sets of information.

The relevance of these designed granular systems thus lies in their capacity to enter continuous cycles of erosion and accretion and to allow for adaptive functional grading on the material macrolevel. Structures that merely change formation can by definition never become redundant. Transitional phases of destabilisation and restabilisation are perceived as productive. These reconfigurations can happen either through deliberate interactions with the system, such as adding or removing granular masses, or through the change of energy in the aggregate due to interaction with its environment. Equally, the specific design of the individual particles and the composition and pouring of the overall aggregate allows for the design of functionally graded matter and differentiated spatial organisations. For example, the level of looseness or adaptability depends on the frictional behaviour of

Jie Ren and Joshua Dijksman, Granular Force Network, Center for Nonlinear and Complex Systems, Duke University, Durham, North Carolina, 2010
left: Granular materials, such as sand, behave in a surprising way: they can flow like a liquid yet carry weight like a solid, which can be studied using photoelastic techniques showing the otherwise hidden and intricate force network between the granules.

The granular material behaves like a solid if the grains are in a comparatively stable state, which means the level of each grain particle's energy is low and the grains are rather stationary relative to each other.

each granule with regards to the forces acting on it. An aggregate that has a high degree of friction will display a higher degree of stability than one without, which makes the overall arrangement less responsive to forces acting on it. Through adjusting friction in an aggregate, the architect can thus prepare for different load situations and ease of reconfiguration. Both these characteristics, which are genuine to granulates, render them novel and relevant to architectural design research.

Designed Aggregate Particles: Programmed Macro-Matter

Aggregate architecture thus implies observing a substance through methods of material and machine computation and interacting with it rather than top-down designing a specific shape and its well-defined and well-placed individual constituents. Yet the behaviour of the aggregate itself can in turn be defined, designed or, rather, fine tuned. Whereas aggregates such as sand or gravel are frequently thought of as occurring naturally, they can also consist of designed particles that can achieve a specific architectural effect of the overall granular arrangement.[3] They are, as it were, programmed macro-matter, where the design objective now lies more in the development of a specific material behaviour through the calibration of its very particles. These are then differentiated to achieve specific system properties and characteristics through closer or looser packing, steeper or lower angles of repose or different degrees of interlocking, density and solidity. The design task has now shifted to the level of the individual particle and the observation of its accumulative effects once larger numbers are set to interact under specific boundary conditions.

The impact of slight variations on the element level to the behaviour and performance on the overall system level can be conceived of as similar to another familiar granular substance: snow. Vast amounts of snow crystals, which are frozen into larger arrangements of snowflakes, assemble to form this granular material.[4] The variant crystal structures on the element level affect the overall quality of snow, be it dense or loosely packed, coarse or fine.[5] As research has shown, many snow types exist, and their behaviour and performance is given by the particular shape of the snow crystal. If an architectural system were to consist of large amounts of crystalline granules, this would allow for a specific and deliberate grading of material properties on a granular level. The morphological differentiation seen in snow crystals can serve as a model of design thinking in aggregate design, as other than in sand, particles are not mainly convex and similar in size and form, but concave and variant.

Material and Machine Computation: Observing the Granulate

Most established design methods and tools in architecture are based on the fundamental understanding of architectural construction as being relatively stable and defined by precisely describing the location of all construction elements both in relation to each other and the overall assembly. Granular materials and aggregate structures cannot be planned this way. They intrinsically require different means of designing, and these means need to be able to capture the distinctive behaviour of granular substances. In contrast to the primacy of assembly systems (defined by shape) in architecture, other disciplines concerned with aggregates (defined by behaviour)

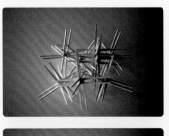

Karola Dierichs, Aggregate Architectures, Institute for Computational Design (ICD), University of Stuttgart, Stuttgart, 2011
Considering manufacturing principles, the particle morphology and aggregate composure of designed granulates are varied in order to test their effect on the overall performance of the system.

Snow Crystals, Electron and Confocal Microscopy Laboratory, Agricultural Research Service, US Department of Agriculture, Beltsville, Maryland, 2008
Depending on temperature and water vapour supersaturation relative to ice, differently shaped snow crystals form, including more or less intricate dendrites as well as hexagonal plates.

have developed both experimental and computational methods for understanding, manipulating and instrumentalising the characteristics of granular substances. Suitable design techniques and technologies for an aggregate architecture can be adopted from these fields that have developed an expertise in observing and interacting with granular substances, as it is precisely this process of observing and interacting that engenders the actual design process.

Both material and machine computation are relevant methodological fields in the investigation of a specific granulate. By this definition computation denotes in its most basic terms the processing and gathering of information, and is thus not limited to digital processes, but also encompasses physical processes that render specific sets of information. Material computation thus denotes methods where a physical substance is set to produce data on the system in question.[6] The computation is based on the innate capacities of the material itself. Machine computation describes methods using a specifically developed algorithm that can be executed by a machine, such as a personal computer. Material and machine computation are based on a common computational model, of information input, information processing and information output.[7]

Material computation in aggregates uses a handful of complementary experimental tools. They are all used in a deliberate manner in order to produce relevant information on the aggregate system. For example, photoelastic materials allow the visualisation of stress distributions.[8] Hence these materials have frequently been used to reveal the network of stress lines in a granulate which otherwise remains unseen and

Material computation in aggregates uses a handful of complementary experimental tools. They are all used in a deliberate manner in order to produce relevant information on the aggregate system.

incomprehensible. These scientific experimental techniques, developed in fields such as geo-engineering, now become the tools of the designer, who starts to tease information out of the system under investigation.[9] They also provide the base for developing related methods for machine computation.

Machine computation offers various mathematical models apt at exploring granular behaviour. Depending on the design task, the designer needs to engage with different mathematical models, the two most widely spread methods being molecular dynamics (MD) or the discrete element method (DEM)[10] on the one hand, and event-driven molecular dynamics (ED) on the other. These two principles apply to very different design tasks: whereas DEM uses a periodic time-stepping and allows for soft particle collisions as well as hard ones, ED simulations are applicable to sparse particle systems with few collisions, as the time model is event-based and allows only for hard collisions.[11] However, rigid body dynamics, a mathematical model implemented in animation software packages, lends itself equally to the simulation of an architectural granulate, since

Karola Dierichs, Aggregate Architectures, Institute for Computational Design (ICD), University of Stuttgart, Stuttgart, 2011
Particles with higher mass retain more heat during rapid cooling than particle samples with very little, leading, respectively, to greater or lesser insulation capacities.

Karola Dierichs, Aggregate Architectures, Institute for Computational Design (ICD) and Florian Fleissner, Institute of Engineering and Computational Mechanics (ITM), University of Stuttgart, Stuttgart, 2011
top: Two different machine computational models, the discrete element method (DEM) and rigid body dynamics, are benchmarked to compare speed and accuracy of the results.

Gerard de Josselin de Jong and Arnold Verruijt, Peter A Cundall and Otto D L Strack, Discrete Element Modelling, Delft/London-Minneapolis, 1969/1979
bottom: Photoelastic images of axially marked discs under strain served to verify the first machine computational model of the discrete element method (DEM).

its strengths lie in the modelling of polygonal rigid particles, a situation encountered in most granulates designed to meet architectural requirements. Discrete simulation Monte Carlo (DSMC) implies an entirely different view of the aggregate, as it does not aim to compute the behaviour of single particles, but rather the probability of the overall arrangement, such as in a pile of sand at relative rest.[12] The deliberate choice of mathematical model then becomes paramount in the process of observational and exploratory design.

For aggregate architectures, material and machine computation need to be understood as integral processes, as the true value of combining them lies in gathering complementary information on the granulate, such as the observation of unlimited amounts of grains in material computation versus the investigation of micromechanical behaviour using DEM methods.[13]

Aggregate Morphology and Performance

An aggregate system can be calibrated and affected on different levels. All of these are aspects of designing with an aggregate, and are thus the tools of the architect working with a granular system. The understanding of the design variables of particle morphology, system composure, pouring and boundary conditions is thus the prerequisite of designing with granular systems. Particle morphology can, for example, vary in size, aspect ratio, packing density and concavity within the constraints set by the production technology. Both injection moulding and flat-sheet production techniques have been tested for their particle-shape-defining characteristics. These variances allow for

calibrating the filling volume, angle of repose, insulation value and friction of the aggregate respectively. In the future, particles could, however, also be produced through a process of self-organisation based on physical behaviour similar to that of snow crystals.

The overall particle system composure is generally referred to as the grading of the system. In a designed architectural aggregate system this aspect allows for the functional grading of the designed material not only with regard to its solidity, stability and load transfer, but also with respect to environmental modulations such as heat conduction, lighting conditions and visual permeability. Pouring processes allow for the control of pouring speed, angle, the distribution of different particle grades as well as pouring paths. Using an industrial six-axis robot allows for a high degree of control of these parameters as well as of the pouring patterns. These pouring processes along with possible additional formwork are the main tools to adjust spatial organisations on different scales of the overall structure.

All of these aggregate system variables allow for calibrating the behaviour of an aggregate architecture in correspondence with the system's three scalar axes of time, space and specificity. The time scales of system changes can be modulated through what in physics are called points of self-organised criticality. Either strategically programmed into the system during the initial pouring process or induced at a later stage, they trigger the transformations from one spatial condition, structural state and environmental performance to another. These reconfigurations can vary in spatial scale from small particle volumes to the entire system. In addition, the spatial scale can also be affected by the

Karola Dierichs, Aggregate Architectures, Institute for Computational Design (ICD), University of Stuttgart, Stuttgart, 2011
below and right: Aggregate structures can be poured using a six-axis industrial robot, the pouring patterns being precisely controlled and the resulting self-solidifying aggregate structures being arranged at very high speed.

opposite bottom: Building-scale structures composed of designed aggregates can be loosely poured and arranged without using formwork, and settle themselves into a stable state.

Karola Dierichs, Aggregate Architectures, Institute for Computational Design (ICD) and Anette Scheider, Institute of Engineering Geodesy (IIGS), University of Stuttgart, Stuttgart, 2011
opposite top: 3-D scanning is used to capture the aggregated structures, and colour coding is used to mark results taken from different standpoints.

aggregate particle's size itself as well as the amount of particles in the overall system, for what might appear like a large particle locally can become small in relation to the global system and vice versa. The degree of specificity can be manipulated through the individual particle geometry, their overall grading and distribution through pouring conditions. Specificity then itself becomes a gradient: a certain area in the aggregate might be modulated to a certain effect in quite a controlled manner, yet this interaction can trigger more emergent phenomena in the wider aggregate field.

Deploying the capacity of loose granular matter, then, implies designing on a particle microlevel rather than on an object macrolevel, designing a material behaviour through its particle composure rather than a static object with permanently placed elements, as well as observing and investigating the granular substance with complementary tools instead of defining a finite form. Rather than being designed, architecture in its specificities then evolves only through its ingredient particles, granulate consistency, pouring and bounding conditions. Aggregate architecture suggests a design paradigm of productive forms of de- and re-stabilisation. Δ

Notes
1. Ralph A Bagnold, *The Physics of Blown Sand and Desert Dunes*, Dover Publications (Mineola, NY), 1954, pp 188–9.
2. Jacques Duran, *Sands, Powders, and Grains: An Introduction to the Physics of Granular Materials, Partially Ordered Systems*, Springer (New York), 2000, p vi.
3. Michael Hensel and Achim Menges (eds), *Morphoecologies*, AA Publications (London), 2006, pp 262–3 and 274–5.
4. Pierre G Rognon, François Chevoir, Hervé Bellot, Frédéric Ousset, Mohamed Naaïm and Phillipe Coussot, 'Rheology of Dense Snow Flows: Inferences From Steady State Chute-Flow Experiments', *Journal of Rheology*, Vol 52 (3), 2008, pp 729–48.
5. François Nicot, 'Constitutive Modelling of Snow As a Cohesive-Granular Material', *Granular Matter*, Vol 6 (1), Springer (Berlin), 2004, pp 47–60.
6. Lars Spuybroek, 'The Structure of Vagueness', in Lars Spuybroek (ed), *NOX: Machining Architecture*, Thames and Hudson (London), 2004, pp 352–9.
7. Susan Stepney, 'The Neglected Pillar of Material Computation', *Elsevier*, Vol 237 (9), 2008, pp 1157–64.
8. Gerard de Josselin de Jong and Arnold Verruijt, ,Étude photo-élastique d'un empilement de disques', *Cahiers du Groupe Français de Rheologie*, Vol 2, 1969, pp 73–86.
9. Sanford Kwinter, 'The Computational Fallacy', in Andrew Marcus, Lauren Kroiz and Christine Gaspar (eds), *Denatured, Thresholds*, Vol 26, 2003, pp 90–2.
10. Peter A Cundall and Otto DL Strack, 'A Discrete Numerical Model for Granular Assemblies', *Géotechnique*, Vol 29 (1), 1979, pp 47–65.
11. Stefan Luding, 'Models and Simulations of Granular Materials', PhD Dissertation No 1996/519, Faculty of Physics, Albert-Ludwigs-University, Freiburg.
12. Thorsten Pöschel and Thomas Schwager, *Computational Granular Dynamics: Models and Algorithms*, Springer (Berlin/Heidelberg), 2005, pp 191–2 and 211–14.
13. Bernard Cambou, Michel Jean and Farhang Radjaï (eds), *Micromechanics of Granular Materials*, ISTE Ltd/John Wiley & Sons Inc (London/Hoboken, NJ), 2009. See also Eric Winsberg, 'A Tale of Two Methods', *Synthese*, Vol 169 (3), 2009, pp 575–92.

Ferdinand Ludwig,
Hannes Schwertfeger
and Oliver Storz

LIVING
SYSTEMS
DESIGNING GROWTH
IN BAUBOTANIK

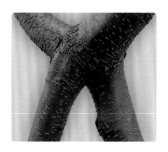

Baubotanik – the construction method that uses living plants for load-bearing in architectural structures – provides a surprising ability to anticipate the latent convergence of non-living and living systems in architecture. Through interdisciplinary research by architects, engineers and biologists it aims to synthesise architectural qualities, constructive requirements and biological properties in living structures. In this article, **Ferdinand Ludwig, Hannes Schwertfeger and Oliver Storz of the Baubotanik research group** at the Institute for Architectural Theory and Design (IGMA) at the University of Stuttgart explain how living and non-living building elements can be designed to develop into vegetal-technical compound structures.

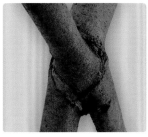

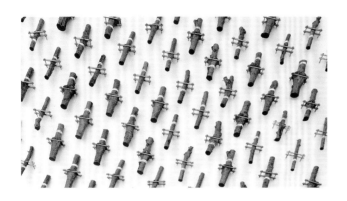

The Baubotanik research group[1] aims at employing the growth processes of living woody plants within architecture, through the integration of design, structural engineering, biological research and horticultural procedures. For designing complex living plant constructions on the scale of fully grown trees, three areas of research need to be investigated. First, a suitable construction material – in this case, living plants with specific characteristics – is required; second, adequate construction techniques need to be developed; and, third, it is essential to work out design rules that are derived from botanical rules of growth. The aim of the Baubotanik research group's various scientific investigations is to set up simple rules to transform trees into hybrid vegetal-technical, load-bearing structures and to develop Baubotanik as a material system that depends on botanical principles and responds to environmental (and social) conditions. The architectural potential of living plant structures can then be explored, with the ecological benefit of tall trees, which usually takes generations, becoming more immediately available.

Designing a Semi-Artificial Organism
Designing a living construction necessitates reconciling constructive and architectural goals with the requirements and characteristics of plants. First, it needs to be acknowledged that the 'production' process does not end with, but rather begins with construction completion, and so an initial configuration and development process needs to be conceptualised. This initial configuration is not only a technical construction, but also the skeletal structure of a baubotanical plant – a living organism that is artificially engineered. Thus baubotanical constructions call for a horticultural way of design thinking and acting.

The basic rule of all natural growth processes – effectiveness – becomes the fundamental design rule. Only if living plant constructions follow this rule will their development meet architects' anticipations. Otherwise plants or plant parts will – sooner or later – die. For instance, the trunks and branches of trees are highly effective pathways for the transport of water and nutrients. If these naturally grown structures are transformed into a framework-like structure, only the shortest connections between roots and leaves show a significant growth in thickness. All indirect connections are less effective and are not needed by the organism – a quite delicate problem when the same parts are needed for other architectural or construction demands.

During growth, trees continuously adapt their outer shape and inner structure to environmental conditions. They especially adapt to mechanical stimuli such as bending forces (caused by wind) and local mechanical pressure (caused, for example, by attached technical components such as steel profiles). In general, trees strive for a structural organisation with an equal distribution of forces on all surface areas. To achieve this goal they show a greater secondary growth in thickness where forces are higher and thus more wood is needed. In this manner they use their resources in an optimised way and follow the rule of effectiveness. When transforming a tree into an artificial framework-like structure, the naturally occurring bending forces (wind loads) are converted into axial tensile and pressure loads and the main force flow occurs in the older wood. Since there are almost no living cells in the axial wood core, the tree is no longer able to optimise its shape in the described manner. It is therefore quite an elaborate challenge to make use of a plant's 'intelligent' growth patterns.

Baubotanical constructions call for a horticultural way of design thinking and acting.

Oliver Storz, Baubotanik research group, The Field, Wald-
Ruhestetten, Germany, 2010
left: Testing field with different geometries of technical components.
The layout of the testing facility is designed to allow a wide variety
of samples to grow, which are used to test the variations of load-
bearing capacities within a time period of three years. *right*: Cross
section of a vegetal-technical joint showing the related changes to
the fibre anatomy of the tree.

Ferdinand Ludwig, Baubotanik research group, Crosswise
Inosculations, Stuttgart, 2010
Crosscuts through a parallel inosculation. The series shows different
developmental stages. In some cases the wooden parts (violet) have
already merged and form a continuous growth ring. In others they
are still separated by the bark tissues.

In conclusion, plants' optimisation of the sap flow as well as
the force flow (hydraulic and mechanical adaptation) leads to a
general design rule for baubotanical constructions. Both the sap
and the force flow have to meet along the same pathways, and
only if this condition is fulfilled will the plants' adaptive growth
processes unfold their full potential for engineering a semi-
artificial organism.

Grafting Physiological Systems: Inosculation Techniques

One of the key techniques of the baubotanik construction
method is to connect plants so that they merge into physiological
units and mechanically strong junctions. Recent experiments by
the Baubotanik research group have examined the applicability
of different joining methods and the impact of the tree
species. The plants were pressed on to each other with various
joining methods, mimicking the natural conditions under
which inosculation (grafting) occurs. Several phases of these
inosculation processes were documented at a macroscopic level
as well as by microscopic cuts. In most cases a mutual enclosing
of the intergrowth partners was observed in the first instance,
before the bark tissues merge on the very position where the two
ingrowth partners meet each other by evolving a callus-like tissue
in the outer bark area. As soon as bigger areas of the bark tissues
have grown together, a partial 'fusion' of their wooden bodies
emerges. A successful inosculation can be proclaimed as soon
as both ingrowth partners share the same annual rings in the
following years.

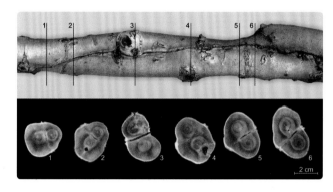

Incorporating Technical Components: Adaptive Growth

In baubotanical structures, not only the plants are connected to
one another – there are also connections between the plants and
technical building elements. To construct these connections, or
joints, the adaptivity of secondary growth is employed: at any
mechanical contact between a tree and another material, the tree
enlarges its surface in order to reduce the increased tension at the
point of contact. During this growth process, a 'form-fit' between
the plant and the technical component develops and the joint
becomes more stable. Technical components with small cross
sections are incorporated within the plants much faster than
those with wider cross sections, and since practice has shown
that the incorporation of technical components also leads to a
predetermined breaking point in the material's structure, it is
essential to reduce this risk by taking care of the stability of the
entire connection during the period of merging.

The form adaptation as described above is an optimisation
at the macroscopic level and is clearly visible in the form-fit.
At the microscopic level, the formation of the plant's wood
fibres is aligned with the flow of forces within the tree. Since
all fibres are orientated perpendicular to the contact surface, the
shape and surface of the extraneous material at each contact
point determines the adjustment of all new growing wooden
fibres. Shear forces in the inner part of the wood are therefore
reduced, which means that under ideal conditions an effect of
'interlocking' between the technical component and the growing
wood is taking place. Under the same conditions, the wood fibres
inside the growing material are pressed on to each other when
load is applied on the joint, which grants even more stability.

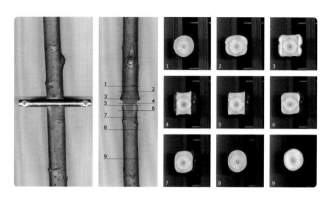

In addition to the flow of forces, there are also 'infrastructural'
aspects affecting the way the growing material is shaped. In
plants, at each joint with construction elements and at each
junction, the interruption or deviation of sap flow affects the
form of the connection. Due to the fact that the initial condition
of all joints and junctions differs slightly, each detail shows
quite an individual growth pattern. A standardised system of
calculating the load-bearing capacities of the whole structural
system is therefore only conceivable on the level of a general
assumption about the future qualities of each detail. Even if this
assumption can be based on statistical data deduced from a wide
range of experiments, definitive conclusions about the status of
the stability of a whole system can only be drawn retrospectively
by comparing them with repeatedly conducted measurements of
the connection's morphology and load tests. Baubotanical load-
bearing systems are always 'systems in a state of becoming'.

Constructing with Living Plants: Material Breeding

Concerning the issue of plant material, it is necessary to develop
and 'produce' living plant stems that fulfil several physiological
and especially morphological and biomechanical prerequisites.
A determining condition is that the plants can be curved in very
tight radii. They should therefore offer a maximum possible
total length, and must also be as thin and flexible as possible.
Through breeding attempts, the Baubotanik research group is
studying how these morphological and biomechanical attributes
can be influenced by divergent growth conditions along with
what kinds of correlations between these qualities and their
anatomic structure exist. Generating specific combinations
of environmental stimuli attempts to increase the slimness
parameter up to the limits of morphological plasticity. As a
sign stimulus, the luminance level and the spectral composition
of the radiation were selected to influence the morphology.
Current results show that plants can be bred with the desired
characteristics particularly by wrapping the stalks. Based on
these experiments, production of baubotanically optimised plant
material could be established in commercial greenhouses.

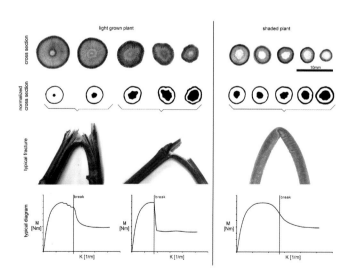

Ferdinand Ludwig and Cornelius Hackenbracht, Baubotanik
research group/Neue Kunst am Ried, Baubotanical Tower,
Wald-Ruhestetten, 2009
Tower time lapse. Development of the Baubotanical Tower in the
first growing season. The sprouting leaves are not just decorative
– they produce the construction material by photosynthesis and
create a 'living facade'.

Intergrowing Vegetal Structures: Plant Addition

As stated above, one of the aims of the Baubotanik research
group is to construct living buildings on the scale of fully grown
trees. One possible technique for doing so is 'plant addition'.
Here, young plants that root in special containers are arranged
in space and connected in such a way that they intergrow in
a vegetal framework structure. Initially, the single plants are
supplied locally with water and nutrients and are held in place by
an espalier-like scaffold. In the course of further developments,
a self-supporting, strong wooden structure can develop by
secondary growth in thickness and the supporting structures
will become obsolete. However, it is first necessary to enable the
transport of water, nutrients and assimilating substances over
the primary borders – from the lowest root up to the top leaves.
Furthermore, the lowest plants, which sit in the ground, must
develop a very powerful root system so that the roots arranged in
the scaffold become obsolete and can be removed together with
the watering and fertilising facilities necessary at the beginning.

The growth pattern of the tropical strangler fig (*Ficus
benghalensis*) is the natural blueprint of this development
process. Individuals of this species cover their need for water and
nutrients 'in the air', which means they grow first epiphytically,
but then shift to a terrestrial growth pattern in the course of their
development. At first they sprout in the crown of a host tree and
send air roots to the ground to exploit the water and nutrient
resources there. The host tree serves as a temporary scaffold,
which is strangled by the air roots. While the host is dying off
and rotting, the air roots form a self-supporting framework-like
structure.

The feasibility of the method has so far been proven by the
Baubotanik research group via a linear plug experiment involving
seven plants. The method was also used on an experimental
structure, the Baubotanical Tower. The vegetal structure of the
building consists of 400 young, 2-metre (6.5-foot) high white
willows (*Salix alba*) that were arranged on seven different levels.
As soon as the living structure is strong enough to support
the ingrown levels and take over the loading capacity, an
unpredictable but expected period of 5 to 10 years, the scaffold
will be removed. The physiological processes of the structure will
be studied as well as the development of the load capacity which
will be proved by weight tests.

Vegetal-Technical Compound Structures: Baubotanik

In general, baubotanical structures can be understood as both a
growing building and a constructed tree. If a constructed tree,
the aesthetic qualities of trees become disposable in the design
process. The differences between nature and growth on the one
hand, and the construction of artefacts on the other, blur. In
naturally developing trees, the emergence of trunk structures
and branching patterns is based on the genetic code of plants
– in baubotanical structures they are partly based on design
processes. Thus the architect has to play at least two new roles –
construction engineer of a 'tree' and designer of a growth process.

In this new role, the architect must consider that the
ecosystem of plants is now playing a major role in the
contextuality of architecture. In consequence, the construction
and structural uses of architecture are strongly tied to
variations that are generated by the ecosystemical factors of the
environment. The influence of the ecosystem can be so strong
that – in extreme cases – the entire existence of a baubotanically
constructed building depends on it.

Indeed, botanically designed support structures can become
more stable by growth in thickness if the construction is based
on the botanical rules of design. However, they can die back
in unexpected places due to inadequate care or inappropriate
environmental conditions. It is therefore crucial to maintain a
practice of design in which 'uncertainty' can affect architecture
in its way of becoming and being, and not just as a side effect
in the process of planning and different construction phases.
This aspect can be read as a problem of engineering or – from
the architect's viewpoint – as a paradigm shift in the way the
idea of 'stability' is understood in principle. Since Baubotanik
is an ecologically embedded architecture, the designer needs
to understand the plant as a profound yet fragile architectural
opportunity.

Fragility as a design strategy was first applied by the Baubotanik research group in 2010. The Platform project contains a temporary structure that supports the young and fragile plants. It is designed in such a way that it can be removed gradually when the plants become more stable through their growth in thickness and begin to develop a supporting function for the entire platform. As such, the temporary structures serve not only to maintain the stability of the platform – they can also be seen as 'stabilisers of expectation'. They inform about the current status of the plants' carrying capacity, but also about the difference between 'expectable' and 'demandable' performance. They are filling the gap of time by emphasising speculation on future growth through the form and modality by which they are constructed.

Through linking the design and construction of botanical hybrid composites to architecture and landscape, technological methods and botanic functions are bound together in forming a hybrid design methodology that gradually turns the idea of a fixed and planned architectural structure into a process of continual becoming. The common method of constructing a system by adding pieces is just the beginning of each baubotanical development. Once all the pieces are assembled the growth process begins and ecologically embeds all baubotanically constructed elements as a semi-artificial organism within its surrounding environment. ◠

Note
1. The interdisciplinary research group Baubotanik was founded by Professor Doctor Gerd de Bruvn at the Institute for Architectural Theory and Design (IGMA) at the University of Stuttgart in 2007. In collaboration with scientists, engineers, humanities scholars and architects the group conducts research on the botanical, constructive and theoretical aspects of building with living plants.

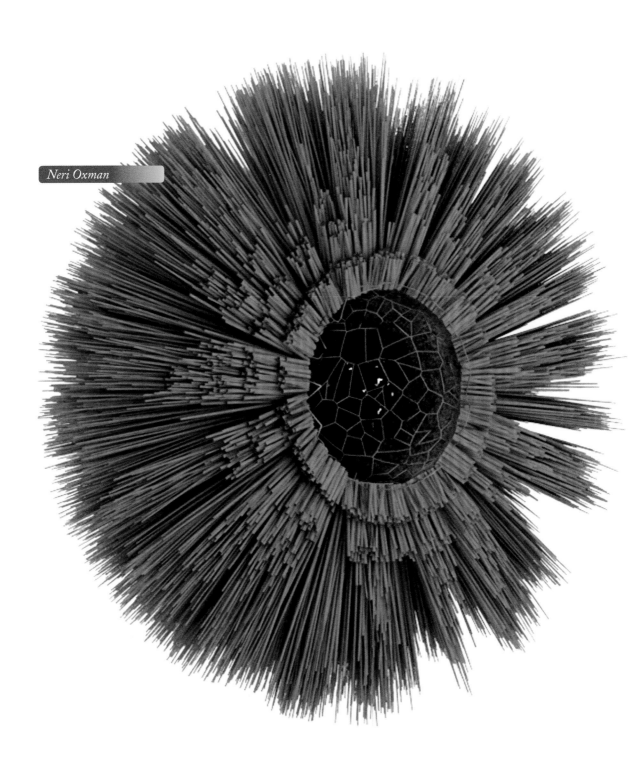

Neri Oxman

PROGRAMMING MATTER

A direct parallel can be made between the Modernist separation of form, structure and material and the more recent tripartite division in digital processes of modelling, analysis and fabrication, which has resulted in the predominance of geometric-driven form-generation. Today, though, design culture is experiencing a shift to a new

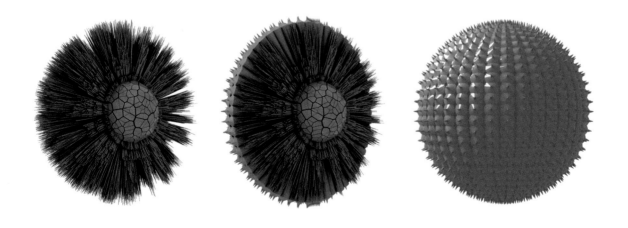

Anthony DeVincenzi and Nicholas Wilkes Polansky, Seed Morphologies, Crafted by Nature, MIT Media Lab, Cambridge, Massachusetts, 2011
Digital models of Plantanus Hybridia and its structural anisotropy demonstrating (left to right from page 88): 1) Seed core; 2) Fibre fill; 3) Achene head packing; 4) Achene shaft; 5) Achene anchor; 6) Core; 7) Core mesh; 8) Finer fill.

level of material awareness. Inspired by nature's strategies where form-generation is driven by maximal performance with minimal resources through local material property variation, **Neri Oxman** investigates a novel design approach to digital fabrication that offers the potential to program physical matter.

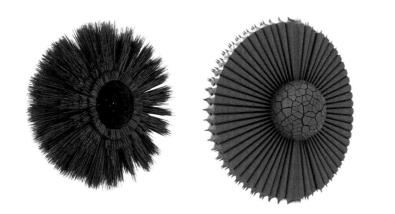

Digital form-finding has been known to support design processes characterised by the control and manipulation of formal elements as a function of the interaction between material and environment. Yet all too often such experiments have resulted in a rather traditional approach to material assignment during processes of fabrication and construction. Indeed, most praxis in the realm of materials in architectural design has centred on questions relating to material selection rather than to material generation. Imagine one could control the spatial distribution of finely grained material elements upon digital fabrication: Can physical matter be made programmable?

Until recently the function of materials in design processes was persistently treated as secondary to form itself. In the context of design materialisation, materials are traditionally predefined and classified as property pools.[1] This condition has been amplified by digital fabrication processes, which have exacerbated the tendency of the designer to materialise design by liberally accessing materials as a library of consistent and physically homogeneous properties.[2] In the natural world, however, materials are rarely homogeneous in shape and composition across a wide range of scales.[3] This is also the reason for the lack of consistently repetitive components in the landscape of the natural environment, contributing to energy conservation and high levels of mechanical efficiency.[4] What makes up nature's secret and how might such logic be emulated in the fabrication of the artificial?

Digital Anisotropy

Materials are traditionally classified by their various properties, as either structural or functional.[5] Structural materials are mainly exploited for their mechanical properties, while functional materials have some other purpose, in relation to electrical, thermal, optical properties, or combinations of them. In nature, however, it is often quite challenging to distinguish between structural and functional materials, as most biological materials such as wood, sponge and bone can be both structural (supporting the branches of a tree or the body) and functional (pumping water up to the leaves or storing energy), with different scales for these different roles. Nature achieves such integration by varying the material's properties and introducing in it directional (structural) changes relative to the structurual, mechanical and environmental functions required. This ability is termed anisotropy. Anisotropy is defined as directional dependency and is expressed as a given difference in a material's physical property[6] when measured along different axes. The directional dependency of a physical property is easily found in most natural materials and is central to the structuring of materials and their behaviours.[7] In the fields of material science and engineering, the concept of anisotropy is tightly linked to a material's microstructure defined by its grain growth patterns and fibre orientation.[8] Beyond these scales, however, anisotropy may be utilised as a design strategy leading away from digital form-finding to trait-finding and the potential programming of physical matter. In design, examples vary depending on the type of property being examined and the manufacturing technology applied to manipulate material organisation. Yet the extent to which anisotropy is explored, as a generative means to create form, is still rather limited and unexplored. If one were able to model anisotropy in the digital space – as part of the form-generation process – what would it look like?

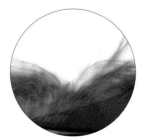

Mathew Blackshaw, Philip R Seaton and Yushiro Okamoto, Feather Morphologies, Crafted by Nature, MIT Media Lab, Cambridge, Massachusetts, 2011
Close-up scan of the feather's generic structure. Barbs have been parted using tweezers following a process of surface formation and self-healing which can be defined as and by geometrical anisotropy.

Early computational models describing geometrical anisotropy in a feather structure exploring four states of hook attachments, from consistently organised to scattered.

Functionally Graded Materials

Functionally graded materials, which are materials with spatially varying composition or microstructure, are omnipresent in nature. A typical cross section of a palm tree reveals radial density gradients corresponding to the bending stiffness instantiated across its height.[9] Such natural materials offer material and structural efficiencies at various length scales.[10] In contrast to natural materials and biological tissues, industrially fabricated constructions, such as concrete pillars, are typically volumetrically homogeneous. While the use and application of homogeneous materials allow for ease of production, many qualities – such as improvements in strength, weight, material usage and functionality – could be obtained by the development and application of functionally graded materials at the product and architectural scales. Below are a few examples from the natural world, by way of defining three classes of anisotropy.

Functionally Gradient Geometrical Anisotropy

The internal structure of a typical feather exhibits the property of anisotropy relative to the function of self-healing. Self-healing is known as the zipping and unzipping mechanism that allows feathers to easily group and ungroup while interfacing with various external environments such as air or water. A typical feather is made of barbs, barbules and barbule hooks providing the structure by which it can cling to a neighbouring feather substructure. The hooks enable barbs to attach to other barb edges in a way that is both surface forming and self-healing. Differences in the degree of the barbules' length, density and overall spatial arrangement lead to differences in type for the overall feather structure, achieved by an anisotropy that can be geometrically described and demonstrated.

Functionally Gradient Structural Anisotropy

The sycamore seed (*Plantanus hybridia*) is made up of several fibre groups, each structured uniquely to cater for its relative function within the overall structure of the seed. This example illustrates the property of anisotropy that is structurally defined and demonstrated. The seed's matter is homogeneous in property; however, it is the way in which the fibre is distributed, its spatial orientation and material characteristics, that generate multiple, distinctly defined micro- and meso-structures within its functional unit.

Functionally Gradient Material Anisotropy

Abundant among cellular solids and many natural materials, functionally gradient material anisotropy is characterised by spatial heterogeneity. Sponges, like bone tissue, demonstrate such properties. They control the flow of water by various combinations of wholly or partially closing the oscula and ostia – their intake pores – as they correspond with underwater external stimuli. The structure of a typical dried sponge reveals the uneven distribution of holes generating a continuous lightweight tissue with varying degrees of density and porosity. Given the significant potential of the ability to design and fabricate building components with varied properties (density, elasticity, translucency) supporting the integration of functions such as load-bearing and natural ventilation, there is value in developing a modelling and fabrication environment for functionally graded products of industrial application and architectural scale.

Functionally Graded Digital Fabrication

Current manufacturing and construction technologies,

bottom left: Microscopic digital video (shot at approximately 20x and 400x) reveals the self-healing and surface-formation process in feathers, guided by geometric anisotropy. The process involves large numbers of tiny, relatively rigid hooks that are attached to flexible barbules, as they interact with the unhooked barbs on the 'paired' feather strand. When pulling the strands apart, the feather's barbs appear to 'unzip'; while local deformations occur during the unzipping process, the feather readily returns to its more relaxed state, allowing it to 'rehook' when barbs are jostled slightly against their mates. This combination of flexibility and rigidity produces a unique resiliency in the feather at a macroscopic scale.

below: CT scans of *Plantanus hybridia* illustrating the various cell structures defined by fibre anisotropy that make up the seed.

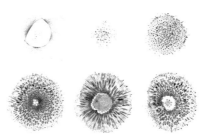

Anthony DeVincenzi and Nicholas Wilkes Polansky, Seed Morphologies, Crafted by Nature, MIT Media Lab, Cambridge, Massachusetts, 2011
bottom right: Electron-microscopy images of *Plantanus hybridia* demonstrating the seed core and mesh structure providing a frame for fibres and spokes. These two distinct structural systems are made from a consistently uniform material, structured uniquely to accommodate distinctive functions. Image generated and processed by Anthony DeVincenzi and Nicholas Wilkes Polansky.

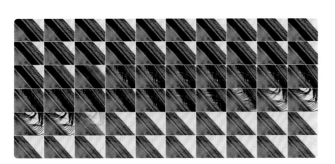

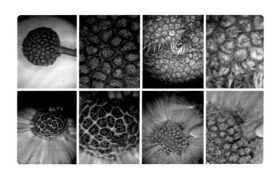

specifically additive manufacturing platforms, are limited in their capacity to represent graduated material properties. Their basic strategy is typically to assign material properties to preshaped building components such as concrete columns or fibreglass panels.[11] Within the design process, this translates into assigning a material property to predefined solids or closed-surface polygons.[12] Both computer-aided design (CAD) tools and industrial fabrication processes (CAM) are thus not set up to represent graduation and variation of properties within solids, such as varied density in concrete, varied elasticity in rubber or varied translucency in glass. As a result, the design process is constrained to the assignment of discrete and homogeneous material properties to a given shape.[13]

Functionally graded digital fabrication is a general approach to the design of structural components with graduated properties. The technical platform is comprised of an automated tool able to dynamically mix and vary the ratios of different component materials in order to produce complex continuous gradients in monolithic structures. Two separate examples of this approach are currently being developed at MIT's Mediated Matter Research Lab: a variable-density concrete system and a variable-elasticity polymer system.[14]

Variable Density Digital Fabrication

The work at MIT is motivated by the hypothesis that density gradients in structural building components made of concrete may increase the strength of a structural component while reducing material waste. The work in progress includes the rapid fabrication of variable-density cement foams, with prototypes illustrating foams of varying densities using aluminium powder admixtures. The work is inspired by load-induced variable densities found in cancellous bone and by radial-gradient densities found in palm tree stems. Palm trees maintain a roughly uniform diameter along their height by thickening the cell walls in certain regions, producing radial density gradients across the surface and volume area of the stem. Measured foam data agrees well with existing data on cement foams made with a protein-based foaming agent.[15]

The project also looks into the controlled automation of density gradients in concrete using a robotic platform. Through the use of a dynamic mixing chamber and an extrusion head mounted on a robotic arm, concrete with controllable density can be 3-D printed.[16] The use of a six-axis robotic arm offers complete positional and angular control of the extruder head, generating interesting fabrication possibilities utilising a set-up similar to current fused deposition modelling technologies. Additional material properties, such as aggregate ratios and optical properties, can also be controlled through dynamic mixing.

Variable Elasticity Digital Fabrication

In many biological systems, the physical properties of the materials are determined by the chemical composition and microstructure of the material's matrix. In soft collagenous tissues such as cartilage, the mechanical behaviour of the matrix is determined by the amount and crimp of the collagen it contains.[17] Experimentally, increased ratios of collagen to proteoglycan in the cartilage matrix correspond to higher tensile moduli.[18] The work at MIT uses polymer mixtures that, when combined in different ratios, produce blends with broad ranges of customisable mechanical properties.

By controlling the ratios in which two or more polymers are mixed immediately prior to deposition and UV curing, monolithic structures with functional gradients can be

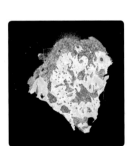
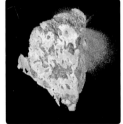

David Lakatos, Cara Liberatore and Marshall Prado, Sponge Morphologies, Crafted by Nature, MIT Media Lab, Cambridge, Massachusetts, 2011
left: CT scan of a typical sponge structure highlighting regions of various densities across the surface and volume area of the scan.

Steven Keating and Timothy Cook, Variable-Density Printing, Mediated Matter Group, MIT Media Lab, Cambridge, Massachusetts, 2011
below: Radial density in palm tree stem (right); variable density in cement (left).

produced using additive fabrication technologies. The current work focuses on automating the controlled mixing and deposition of polymer layers using a six-axis robotic arm, as well as integrating the physical fabrication platform with user design interfaces.

Functionally graded digital fabrication is a novel design approach offering the potential to program physical matter. Its technological method enables dynamically mixing and varying the ratios of component materials in complex 3-D distributions in order to produce continuous gradients in 3-D fabricated objects. This expands the potential of prototyping, since the varying of properties allows for optimisation of material properties relative to their structural and functional performance, and for formal expressions directly and materially informed by environmental stimuli.

This approach could potentially contribute to efficient conservation of material usage, high performance of integrated structures, optimised response to mechanical stimuli, and overall improved product life spans. It is anticipated that in parallel to the emerging capabilities of multimaterial, free-form fabrication, materials with a wide range of mechanical, electrical, thermal and optical properties will soon be seamlessly fabricated. Indeed, traditional CAD programs are inadequate in efficiently utilising this vast design potential. The MIT research outlines an approach for programming matter and demonstrates the first steps in rendering physical the digital design substrate. Through a new fabrication approach supporting continuous property gradients within structural form, designers can meet high-level functional goals while creating new expressions in nature's dialect. ⌂

Notes
1. S Vogel, *Comparative Biomechanics: Life's Physical World*, Princeton University Press (Princeton, NJ), 2003.
2. N Oxman, 'Structuring Materiality: Variable Property Fabrication of Heterogeneous Materials', ⌂ *The New Structuralism: Design, Engineering and Architectural Technologies*, Vol 80, No 4, 2010, pp 78–85.
3. LJ Gibson, MF Ashby and BA Harley, *Cellular Materials in Nature and Medicine*, Cambridge University Press (Cambridge), 2010.
4. N Oxman, 'Material-Based Design Computation: Tiling Behavior', *ACADIA 09: reForm Building a Better Tomorrow, Proceedings of the 29th Annual Conference of the Association for Computer Aided Design in Architecture*, 2009.
5. Ibid.
6. Ie, absorbance, refractive index, etc.
7. L Gibson and M Ashby (1999), *Cellular Solids: Structure and Properties,* Cambridge University Press (Cambridge), 1999.
8. LJ Gibson, 'The Mechanical Behaviour of Cancellous Bone', *Journal of Biomechanics* 18 (5), 1985, pp 317–28.
9. PM Rich, 'Mechanical Structure of the Stem of Arborescent Palms', *Botanical Gazette* 148 (1), 1987, pp 42–50.
10. C Ortiz and MC Boyce, 'Bioinspired Structural Materials', *Science* 319 (5866), 2008, p 1053.
11. E Sachs and M Cima et al, 'Three-Dimensional Printing: the Physics and Implications of Additive Manufacturing', *CIRP Annals-Manufacturing Technology* 42 (1), 1993, pp 257–60.
12. W Sheng, N Xi, H Chen, M Song and Y Chen, 'Surface Partitioning in Automated CAD-Guided Tool Planning for Additive Manufacturing', IEEE International Conference on Intelligent Robots and Systems, Las Vegas, 2003.
13. N Oxman, 'Variable Property Rapid Prototyping', *Virtual and Physical Prototyping* 6 (1), 2011, pp 3–31.
14. The work included in this article has been partly the product of a course entitled: Crafted by Nature, taught by the author and assisted by Ari Kardasis (MIT Computation Group).
15. T Tonyan, *Mechanical Behavior of Cementitious Foams*, MIT Press (Cambridge, MA), 1991.
16. N Oxman, 'Methods and Apparatus for Variable Property Rapid Prototyping', Google Patents. 2010.
16. A Markworth and K Ramesh et al, 'Modelling Studies Applied to Functionally Graded Materials', *Journal of Materials Science* 30 (9), 1995, pp 2183–93.
17. AK Williamson and AC Chen et al, 'Tensile Mechanical Properties of Bovine Articular Cartilage: Variations with Growth and Relationships to Collagen Network Components', *Journal of Orthopaedic Research* 21 (5), 2003, pp 872–80.
18. N Oxman, 'Variable Property Rapid Prototyping', op cit.

Material tests for a concrete extruder head capable of dynamic density and aggregate control. Mechanical foaming techniques are automated using a six-axis robotic arm to produce lightweight, floating concrete structures with programmable porosity. The image illustrates a linear density gradient in a concrete sample with the centre of gravity highlighted by the pivot point produced by varying the ratio of foaming agent.

David Lakatos, Cara Liberatore and Marshall Prado, Sponge Morphologies, Crafted by Nature, MIT Media Lab, Cambridge, Massachusetts, 2011
Initial concept models demonstrating geometrical, structural and material anisotropy mimicking the natural sponge. The top images show the fabrication set-up for the physical modelling of the sponge system which is based on a sealed watertight container into which inflatable units of various volumes are inserted, constricting the sponge's external membrane form. An additional internal distribution set-up of inflatable bodies determines the spatial porosity across the volume area of the system. The bottom image illustrates material density variation across unit cells within the sponge system. Variations in strength, density and elasticity are achieved by programming the spatial distribution of elastic material.

Steven Keating, Variable-Density Fabrication, Mediated Matter Group, MIT Media Lab, Cambridge, Massachusetts, 2011
Image demonstrating the six-axis 3-D printing capabilities of the robotic platform. The code developed for this platform allows the designer to take a 3-D part file, slice it into layers and paths, and convert it into a robotic industrial operating language. The image demonstrates initial results using various test extruder heads such as a silicone extruder and an ABS plastic extruder in 0.3-millimetre layer thickness with an accuracy of 0.02 millimetres.

Image demonstrating the robotic arm platform acting as a six-axis 3-D printer for the digital fabrication of variable elasticity gradients in product design scales.

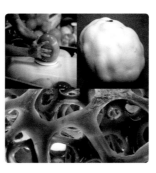

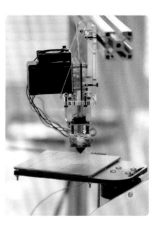

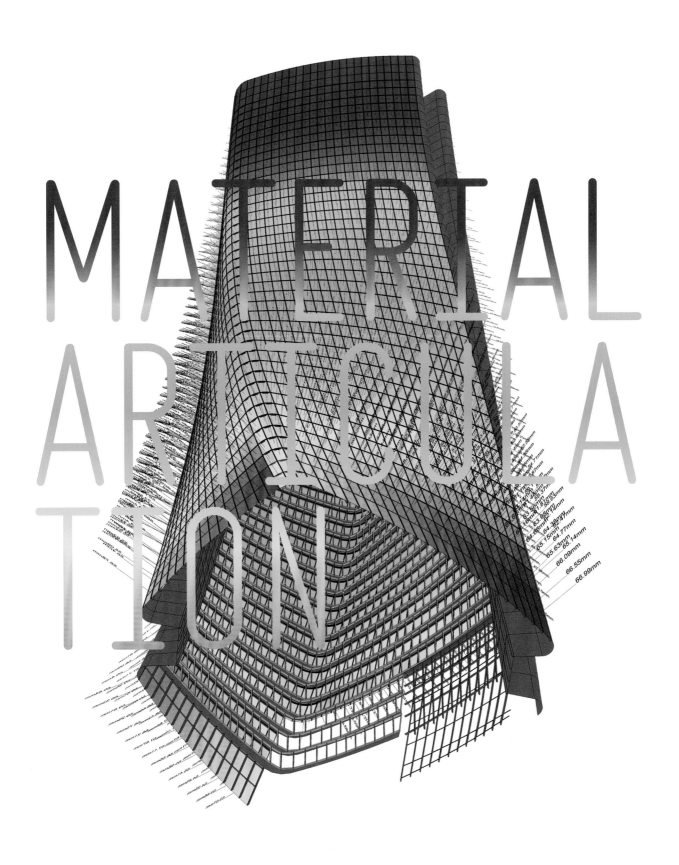

MATERIAL ARTICULATION

COMPUTING AND CONSTRUCTING CONTINUOUS DIFFERENTIATION

Free-form geometric designs make use of continuously differentiated components that exist within a multidimensional envelope of material performance, fabrication capabilities, logistics and cost. In this article, **Cristiano Ceccato** explains how geometric form-rationalisation and analysis of constructability at the functional as well as the computational level form the basis for achieving advanced designs in terms of articulation of material through mass-customised industrial production. Taking examples from the current work of Zaha Hadid Architects (ZHA), he presents a necessarily evolving framework of computational design and associated practice of architecture that is attempting to close the gaps between computational design, digitally controlled manufacturing and evolving mechanisms of contemporary construction and project delivery.

Zaha Hadid Architects, City Life Tower, Milan, 2011

Complex geometry has long existed in architecture. Most new claims of a new design language are, in fact, mostly the revisiting of expressive formalisms that have been extensively explored in the past: from the Solomonic columns of St Peter's baldachin in Rome (1623–34) by Gianlorenzo Bernini, to the Sagrada Família in Barcelona (1833–) by Antoni Gaudí; and from Eladio Dieste's sinusoidal walls of the Atlántida Church in Uruguay (1958–60) through Pier Luigi Nervi's Palazzetto dello Sport in Rome (1956–7) to Eero Saarinen's JFK (1956–62) and Dulles (1958–62) airport terminals, to name but a few, complex geometry has found its physical expression in constructed architecture over hundreds of years, each design mirroring the available construction methods of its time. What is different and new today is the unique opportunity that the advent of digital technology presents to the architect: the ability to codify a design as an algorithmic expression of purely geometric and mathematical constructs, allowing a precision of form-generation and a speed of its exploration that were previously unimaginable. This presents a problem: the speed of form-exploration has accelerated beyond the speed of maintaining an adequate complementing execution process, which can no longer keep, and thus destabilises, the relationship of confidence that must necessarily exist between architect and client.

During the early 1990s, a number of architectural theorists and researchers including John Frazer, Karl Chu and others pioneered the application of natural growth, evolutionary differentiation and morphogenetic processes to the production of architectural form and spatial logic.[1] These experiments combined sophisticated algorithmic computation with biologically derived search and optimisation techniques, as well as the application of different forms of artificial intelligence to produce complex 'design systems' with self-regulating morphogenetic characteristics and emergent behaviour. In most cases, the geometric and spatial constructs emerging from this work were not intended as literal architectural form, but rather as visualisations of data structures that embodied a particular architectural logic that would form the framework for a particular design downstream.

Over the past decade, this pioneering work has been systematically disseminated at countless universities and has progressively taken root in the applications of design and architecture practice worldwide. With this broadening of digital inquiry comes both a dilution of the original rigour of research and a desire to apply this thinking more directly to architectural work. The theoretical musings of algorithmic form-generation have given way to the preoccupation of execution, and therein lies the challenge: how to achieve a complete digital life cycle of architecture, whereby a computation design process dovetails seamlessly with a digital execution framework, and how to capture innovative fabrication and construction processes such that they are both driven by the upstream digital design process, while in turn informing the very same design process on their capabilities, constraints, and so-called best practices.

The Quest for a Constructible Rationale

'Pre-rationalisation' is also referred to as designing with 'first principles', using a set of given geometric rules and methods to produce a solution that is constructible from the outset. These rules may incorporate parameters of manufacturability,

Zaha Hadid Architects, Galaxy SOHO, Beijing, 2012
3-D BIM cladding tender model showing sample panel families at the outer fascia bands. Families are coloured identically; double-curved individual panels are in pink.

'Pre-rationalisation' is also referred to as designing with 'first principles', using a set of given geometric rules and methods to produce a solution that is constructible from the outset. These rules may incorporate parameters of manufacturability, material performance, acceptable functional minima and

maxima, and, often, an understood range of cost implications. Such first principles, or rules and parameters, are not necessarily immediately understood, but rather may emerge from a conventional trial-and-error design process through which a particular architectural aspiration may be pursued.

material performance, acceptable functional minima and maxima, and, often, an understood range of cost implications. Such first principles, or rules and parameters, are not necessarily immediately understood, but rather may emerge from a conventional trial-and-error design process through which a particular architectural aspiration may be pursued. Early families of rules and parameters may in turn inform the architectural concept itself, and so on. It is the architect's responsibility, in this case, to ensure that the methods and rules that are available adequately implement the solution to a particular architectural challenge – the formal aesthetics often emerge from the application of the rules and principles themselves.

Fundamentally, a pre-rationalised process embeds the necessary assembly constraints and design logic into its constituent geometric rules, such that only constructible designs can be produced by the system. This presents an enormous advantage in that the outcome of the downstream design development and construction phases are technically predictable and the cost controllable. Modifications or enhancements to the rules may be selectively introduced whereby design variants may be generated that provide a greater range of solutions while maintaining control of the design. The result is the embodiment of a complex form through a finite set of components, which may be a series of identical parts that can be assembled to produce a complex form, or families of self-similar components that have a common geometric topology and constructional typology and differ mainly in their individual geometric dimensions. By keeping the manufacturing techniques and assembly methods the same across the components, the cost and schedule of a project may be further controlled. Such pre-rationalised design strategies have been exemplified through a broad range of works by firms such as Skidmore, Owings & Merrill (SOM), Foster + Partners, Kohn Pedersen Fox (KPF) and, more recently, Wilkinson Eyre Architects.

'Post-rationalisation' is a contrasting approach that seeks to provide a solution of constructability to a formal design that is initially developed more for its formalistic expression than a preset solution of buildable rules. Form-finding in this case is understood differently: the process is driven by aesthetic concerns, and a shape may be produced by a variety of means, but without pre-empting its method of construction or geometric language. Firms such as Gehry Partners have used this method with highly successful results. In Gehry's work, an inherent rationale is often applied through the use of physical models, whereby the curving and folding of sheets of card mimic the material behaviour of sheet metal quite faithfully, the latter being a favourite material of choice of that firm. Implicitly, the mathematical concept of the developable surface ($C_{Gauss} = 0$) is embedded into the geometric materiality of the paper model and scales reasonably well to the full-scale architectural cladding artefact. In this case, the computer serves as a means to capture the initial gestures and refine the underlying geometry – in Gehry's words, to 'catch the curve, not create it'.[2]

In the work of Zaha Hadid Architects (ZHA), the post-rationalisation step complements the digital free-form design processes arising from the use of tools such as subdivision surface modelling in Maya. In this case, the interplay between a fluid, dynamic design language that is deliberately unconstrained by premature concerns of constructibility, and the sensitive

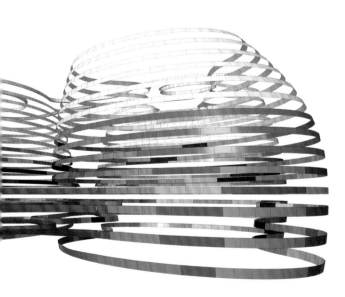

application of rationalisation techniques that are faithful to the original form, have enabled the firm to explore radically different design geometries and accurately execute them within a framework of cost, contractual framework and local context of fabrication and construction quality – all of which vary dramatically across regions and are thus of paramount importance for a firm committed to worldwide practice.

Material Computation: Embedding Physical Constraints into Digital Form-Generation

The advent of parametric design technology and the introduction of constructive solid geometry (CSG) modellers software tools into the architecture, engineering and construction industry is heralding what could be described as one of the 'Holy Grails' of digital architecture and design computation: the concept of 'co-rationalisation', in other words the embedding of material properties and assembly constraints directly into the (parametric) design model at the design stage, such that either the geometric definition of the model or the rules that describe its constructibility may be altered in real time within the parametric model. In other words, the combination of parametric geometry and material constraint definitions permit the creation of an integrated design system that allows the designer to broadly explore design options without losing the critical properties of constructibility and fabrication constraints that are embedded within the model.

In practice, this can be achieved in a number of ways. The more sophisticated parametric tools available today include decision-making nodes that allow the model to have a certain degree of 'intelligence', in the sense that, depending on real-time modifications to the geometry, the parametric construct of the model can react by modifying the detail assemblage according to different rules based on particular decision trees. For example, in the CATIA system these are referred to as 'checks', 'rules' and 'reactions', and constitute a form of user-defined artificial intelligence (in the classic computer science definition of AI) that can be used to govern the detailing of a design within a finite set of possible outcomes.

Another form of co-rationalisation can be achieved by overlaying different layers of parametric models on top of each other, each new model reading the geometry of the previous and implementing a further level of rationalisation itself, and yet being able to respond to any geometric updates of its predecessor in real time. An example of this is the Galaxy SOHO project by ZHA, which was developed initially as a Maya subdivision surface model that acts as the main 'driving' geometry for a series of overlaid models in CATIA, each of which brings a higher level of geometric definition and constructibility for fabrication and assembly than the previous one.

In this particular project, the developable surface mentioned above is the key geometric device to achieving a constructible cladding geometry that is equally achievable in technical terms, is affordable within financial constraints, yet aesthetically pleasing. However, unlike the post-rationalisation process of selectively fitting developable surface geometry to a predefined design shape, in the Galaxy SOHO project the ZHA team built the developable surface definition directly into the parametric models that define the detailed shape of the building itself. In other words, the team was able to apply modifications to the

Zaha Hadid Architects, Galaxy SOHO, Beijing, 2012
below: Vertical fascia production model. Naming, unfolding and the setting out of panels was fully automated, enabling the team to reiterate the design several times without affecting the implied workload per iteration.

centre: The setting out of the panels was by floor level, with one A0 sheet per floor and tower. Scripts were developed to select, reorient and unfold each floor's facade panels.

bottom: Automatically generated A0 tender sheet including the setting out and naming of panels. Workflow was established and automated; 144 drawings were generated in 35 minutes.

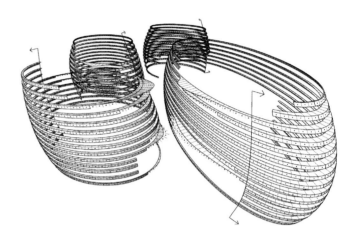

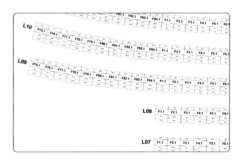

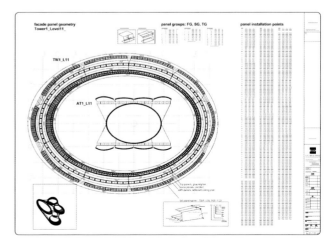

Zaha Hadid Architects, Wangjing SOHO, Wangjing, Beijing, 2012
centre: Facade panels blend in three different ways: height, slope and skew. Panel twist and joint alignment are governed by the level of panel skew. If the skew is ignored, the panel twist increases beyond the material elasticity of aluminium.

bottom: Raw analysis of panel inclination (black), skew (red) and principal curvature radius (blue). This data is a departure point for the internal workings of the facade generator.

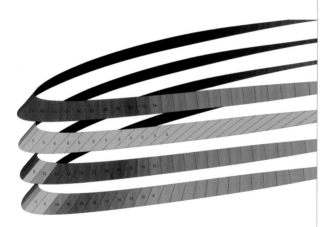

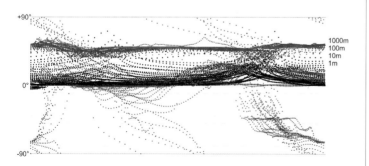

design during the upstream design iterations of the project while already being able to ascertain its constructibility downstream, and understand the range of building components that could be built within such rules, as opposed to simpler (flat) or more complex and expensive (double-curved) elements.

The developable surface model itself was then overlaid with a further parametric model that reduced complexity by implementing self-similar families of identical panels that implement conical geometry across different levels. Keeping within a limit of visually perceptible deviation from the original surface forms, the resulting model of continuously differentiated conical and developable surfaces presents a 'best fit' implementation of the original double-curved design within achievable parameters of constructibility (supplied by the fabricators) and cost (dictated by the client). The final iteration of this sequence of parametric co-rationalised models in turn forms the basis for the development of downstream shop drawings by the contractors. The underlying parametric infrastructure ensures that while not desirable, late-stage modifications to the design may be incorporated into the model definition.

This type of rationalisation and computational constructibility has also been employed in other ZHA projects. The Wangjing SOHO project, for the same client, revisited the problem of the rationalisation of double-curved surfaces through sheet metal, but with much more stringent requirements in terms of cost and fabrication complexity. In this case, a different, but closely related, technique was used, whereby the requirements for the panel geometry were directly encoded in a panel-generation VB script in Rhino, which would analyse the local curvature condition of the underlying original double-curved 'driver surface' and generate families of related flat and single-curved panels within a given geometric solution space. Another high-rise project, City Life in Milan, uses similar analytical scripting techniques for the assessment of out-of-plane warping of unitised glazing panels, which are then verified with the fabricator's guarantee limits for cold-bending glass in curtain-wall manufacturing. In each of these cases, a downstream digital design process embeds specific material computation within the geometric solution, ensuring a constructible outcome to an upstream formal digital design.

Focusing the Lens: Articulating the Need for an Integrated Practice

Much has been made in recent times of the return of the 'master builder' and the re-empowerment of the architect as the master controller of project data, in particular through tools such as building information modelling (BIM). However, this will not suffice if the client's confidence in the architect's capability of executing their design is not maintained. The solution space described above represents an agreed cost and constructibility framework between architect and client, such that the architect is aware of the geometric 'playing field' for the project, and the client is assured a risk-controlled digital data set for tender that allows them to tender the project with confidence in terms of managing the price range of the contractors' tender returns. In this sense, a tight, collegial total collaboration between client, architect and contractor is necessary for the advancement of architecture to succeed. In the case of the Galaxy SOHO project,

Zaha Hadid Architects, City Life Tower, Milan, 2011
Facade analysis of the tower. An integrated parametric set-up via a VB Rhino script for the underlying geometry and analysis enabled rapid testing of variations on the overall twist and out-of-plane deviation per glazing panel and the resulting warp on the facade panels. These variations provided not only quick conceptual form studies, but also evaluation against manufacturing criteria for cold-bending of glass at the same time.

Zaha Hadid Architects, Wangjing SOHO, Wangjing, Beijing, 2012
below: Analysis of the generated panels. As a result of controlled skew blend, the colour-coded twist per panel stays moderate and within the cold-bending capacity of the facade's aluminium sheets.

Zaha Hadid Architects, Galaxy SOHO, Beijing, 2012
bottom: 3-D BIM construction coordination model showing structure, MEP and courtyard cladding. The model is used continuously during construction for verifying coordination and 3-D shop drawings.

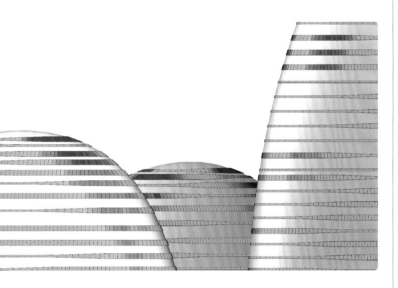

this implied a learning curve on both sides, developing new practices together in terms of establishing a joint framework for the development of the design, from its computation through to coordination and the issuance of the 3-D geometry model as part of the tender contract for the project.

For architects in practice, the biggest challenge today is the translation of complex forms into built artefacts that do justice to the original design inception while trying to reconcile advanced forms of digital design with comparatively archaic methods of procurement, fabrication and construction. Concepts such as 'file to fabrication' and 'digital manufacturing' are meaningless and have no effect on practice if the legal framework of contract scope and liability is not understood – the risk being the architect relegated to 'design consultant', perhaps within a design-build contract where design ambition and quality frequently lose out to value engineering and risk minimisation by the contractor. At the same time, the integration of computation as the core mechanism for the design and production of architecture cannot be separated from the required legal frameworks and professional mechanisms of practice. In order to consider the integration of process necessary to implement a unified architecture, it is therefore necessary to continue to critique, dismantle and reconstruct such frameworks as integrated digital architecture practice spanning the complete life cycle of design, engineering, procurement and delivery. ∆

Concepts such as 'file to fabrication' and 'digital manufacturing' are meaningless and have no effect on practice if the legal framework of contract scope and liability is not understood

Notes
1. JH Frazer, *Themes VII: An Evolutionary Architecture,* Architectural Association (London),1995; and KS Chu (XKavya), 'Modal Space: the Virtual Anatomy of Hyperstructures', in M Pearce and N Spiller (eds), *∆ Architects in Cyberspace,* Profile 118, 1995.
2. M Sorkin, *Some Assembly Required,* University of Minnesota Press (Minneapolis, MN), 2001, p 97.

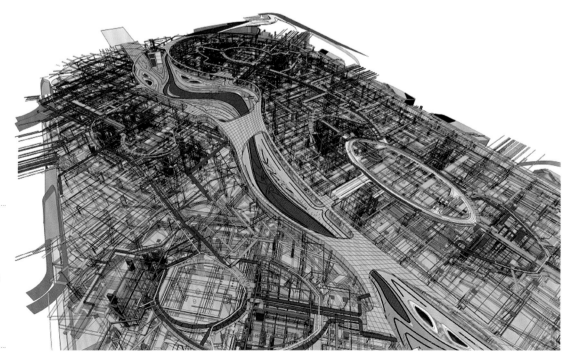

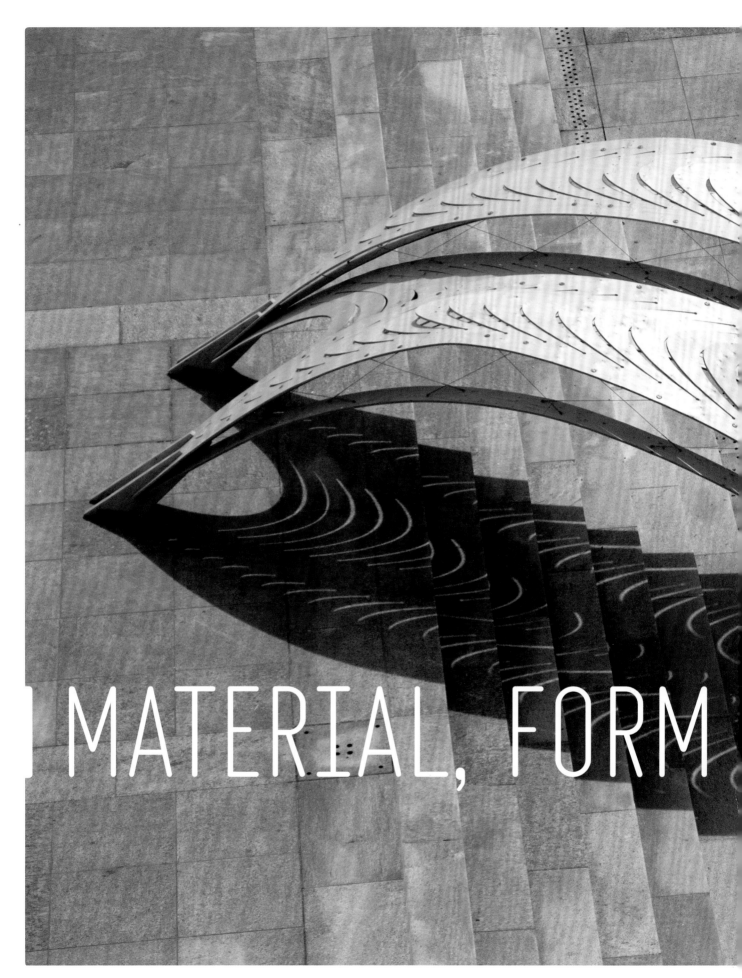

MATERIAL, FORM

Toni Kotnik and Michael Weinstock

Conventionally, material in architecture has been treated as the 'servant' of form. An iterative design process, though, that continuously integrates material, form and force has the potential to unfold a new generative logic of form-finding. This offers ways of processing the flow of forces through a material object and balancing variations of form with the organisation and behaviour of material. **Toni Kotnik and Michael Weinstock** present a series of experimental construction projects, developed within the Emergent Technologies and Design (EmTech) programme at the Architectural Association (AA) in London, that explore the intricate relationship between material, form and force.

Architectural Association Emergent Technologies and Design Programme (AA EmTech) and Chair of Structural Design research unit at the Swiss Federal Institute of Technology Zurich (ETH Zurich), AA/ETH Pavilion, Science City Campus, ETH Zurich, 2011
above: The temporary installation in front of the ETH Zurich architecture department building.

left: The pavilion functions primarily as sun shading for parts of the stairs in front of the architecture department building. The construction is based on the bending behaviour of large 11 x 2.5 metre (36 x 8.2 foot) sheets of 18-millimetre (0.7-inch) thick plywood and spans about 8 metres (26 feet).

AND FORCE

Every physical being, living and non-living, has to support its materiality against the various forces that are imposed upon it by its environment, such as gravity, wind or atmospheric pressure. Philosophically speaking, the materiality of physical beings can be thought of as embodiment of two intrinsic coincident principles: primary matter itself and its form, its gestalt in space.[1] Both principles are intricately interwoven, and in the physical world one cannot occur without the other: no material is without form and no form exists without materialisation.

The Primacy of Form

Traditionally, however, the discourses within architecture and the visual techniques of architectural design practice have privileged form over material, with material rarely examined beyond its aesthetic properties or its technological capacities to act as a servant to form. In recent years, this tendency has been reinforced by contemporary methods of digital design with its emphasis on information-driven manipulation of NURBS-geometry within a computational environment, an approach that tends to exclude material from the generative process, leaving the corporal aspects of materiality to the later phases of adapting the designed form as a structure in preparation for fabrication and construction.

More recently, digital simulations of physical form-finding experiments, such as the hanging chain models or tensioned membranes originally used by architects and engineers like Antoni Gaudí, Frei Otto or Heinz Isler, have become commonly available. Both methods produce optimised structural forms from a direct causal relationship between the spatiality of force flow and the generated form. But neither in digital nor in physical form-finding techniques do material properties play a major defining role in the process; material is merely a subordinate means of tracing the form and making it buildable.

More recently, digital simulations of physical form–finding experiments, such as the hanging chain models or tensioned membranes originally used by architects and engineers like Antoni Gaudí, Frei Otto or Heinz Isler, have become commonly available.

In addition, the digital design processes that exclude simulations of physical form-finding in favour of a process of negotiation between architectural and structural demands generally proceed by an integration of structural analysis into the later stages of the generative process. So they too have a similar hierarchical relationship between form and material, and result in a performance-oriented deformation of the initial form with respect to stress fields caused by the flow of forces along the form. In this way of working, the assumed materialisation of the form mediates between the intensity of the force flow and the amount of deformation. As before, the primary focus is on form as the direct resultant of the acting forces.

The Distribution of Material

In all these design approaches, however, it is evident that form cannot be treated independently of material, even when the strongest architectural interest is in form-finding. It is material through which forces flow, and the arrangement of material in space, the pattern of its distribution, directly influences the efficiency of the flow of forces, the direction of the flow and its intensity. This is evident in all living forms. For example, plants resist gravity and wind loads through variation of their stem sections and the organisation of their material in multiple and integrated hierarchies. It is this hierarchical organisation of subtle and continuous changes in material properties that enables plants to respond to both local and global stresses.

Variations in the section and material properties of 'structural elements' in living biological systems offer significant advantages over the constant section that is conventional in engineered structures. Sectional variations produce anisotropy,[2] a gradation of values between stiffness and elasticity along the length of the structural element that is particularly useful for resisting dynamic and unpredictable loading conditions such as those produced by wind. Growth under the continual stresses of the physical environment produces this pattern of organisation of material; the forces that the living organism experiences while it is growing encourage the selective deposition of new material where it is needed and in the direction that it is

opposite left: Due to the size of the plywood sheets, conventional production facilities could not be used. Necessary cuts were therefore carried out along premounted drawings using a stick saw.

below: A transparent structure can be achieved through small variations in the length of the sheets. Cuts help to reduce the bending stiffness of the sheets and allow for increased bending radius, as well as a functional differentiation between the load-bearing arches along the edge of the sheets and the louvre system.

Steel cables act as cross-bracing of the arches and help to evenly distribute additional loads, minimising further deformation of the construction. Five-centimetre (1.96-inch) wide washers transfer the tension forces from the cables into the plywood.

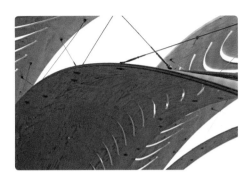

The adaptation of the form and the distribution of material are integrated in living organisms in response to the forces acting upon them. It has been the convention to study and computationally simulate form and material separately, but any adaptation of the form results in the immediate redistribution of matter in space and vice versa.

needed. This process also continues throughout the whole life of the organism whenever changes in stress and load occur.

The formation of reaction wood in trees, needed to realign a trunk towards the vertical when it has experienced inclined growth or to offset loads from prevailing winds, and the mechanisms of bone remodelling, are perhaps the most widely studied examples of responsive distribution and accumulation of material. Reaction wood has a fibre orientation and cellular structure that is different to that of normal wood, and is produced in successive annual rings that vary in width and density as local circumstances require. In bones, material is removed from any areas that are not stressed and deposited in more highly stressed areas. For example, in the femur, the longest and largest bone of the human body, this leads to an accumulation of material at the greater trochanter[3] where forces have to be redirected and, therefore, stresses are the highest. Among all the living forms of nature there are many differing load-bearing architectures, each a response to the specific set of load conditions that they experience. The evolution of all the multiple variations of biological form cannot be thought of as separate from the spatial distribution of material, and it is the integrated hierarchies of material organisation within their form from which their structural performance emerges.

The adaptation of the form and the distribution of material are integrated in living organisms in response to the forces acting upon them. It has been the convention to study and computationally simulate form and material separately, but any adaptation of the form results in the immediate redistribution of matter in space and vice versa. Materialised forms and formed material are complementary principles of materiality – distinguishable, but not dividable. Form and material act upon each other, and this interaction cannot be predicted by analysis of either one of them alone. Contemporary form-driven design approaches do not yet take full advantage of the possibilities offered by a generative system that integrates material, form and force as continuous iterations in the design process. When processing the flow of forces through a material object, and balancing variations of form with the organisation

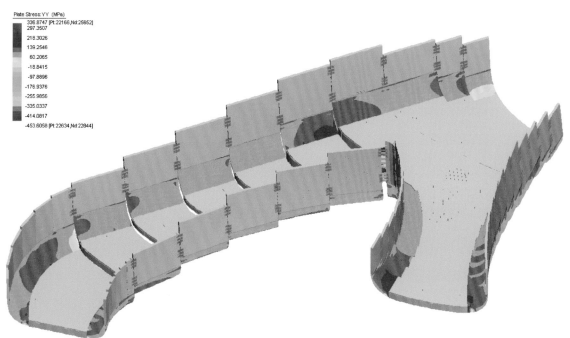

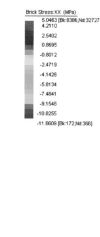

Plate Stress: YY (MPa)

336.8747 [Pt:22166,Nd:25652]
297.3507
218.3026
139.2546
60.2065
-18.8415
-97.8896
-176.9376
-255.9856
-335.0337
-414.0817
-453.6058 [Pt:22634,Nd:22844]

Brick Stress: XX (MPa)

5.0463 [Bk:8386,Nd:32727]
4.2110
2.5402
0.8695
-0.8012
-2.4719
-4.1426
-5.8134
-7.4841
-9.1548
-10.8255
-11.6609 [Bk:172,Nd:366]

The overall arch-like form of the two legs of the bridge has been in part the result of a form-oriented design approach during the initial design phase, with Gaudí's hanging chain model as precedence.

Architectural Association Emergent Technologies and Design Programme (AA EmTech) and the Institute for Computational Design (ICD), University of Stuttgart, Bifurcated Bridge, Architectural Association, London, 2010
Even stress distribution along the components in the final design development. The highest stress occurs at the transition from horizontal to vertical elements, which is at the area of redirection of the force flow.

opposite: Final design of bridge component with fully developed differentiation of the cross section. The vertical section of the component consists of 40-millimetre (1.59-inch) of ply, the horizontal walkway has been separated into two layers of 5-millimetre (0.19-inch) ply with additional ribs for stiffening. These two planar surfaces are connected by a curved solid timber inlay in the area of transition from horizontal to vertical section. Further stiffening of the U-shaped bridge component is provided by the solid timber handrail and the solid edge at the top part of the component.

and behaviour of material, the emergent form has the capacity to respond effectively to forces that will be imposed upon it in the physical world. This balancing of material, form and force is the focal point of a recent series of projects conducted within the Emergent Technologies and Design (EmTech) programme at the Architectural Association (AA) in London.

The Pavilion

In collaboration with the Chair of Structural Design research unit of the Swiss Federal Institute of Technology Zurich (ETH Zurich), a temporary light timber construction has been designed that functions as sun shading for parts of the grand stairs in front of the ETH architecture department. It is based on bending behaviour under self-weight of oversized sheets of plywood of up to 11 x 2.5 metres (36 x 8.2 feet).[4] The design activates the material properties as the defining element in the transfer of forces, and the design method is related to the hanging chain model. The resulting form, however, is not achieved as a pure geometry of force independent of material as the chain model is, but instead as a direct reaction of the material to the forces acting upon it. Cuts within the sheets influence their bending resistance and so enable a larger spatial enclosure and reduced wind load acting upon the structure, additionally producing a shadow pattern on the stairs, which are used as a seating area during the summer. Varying the length of the sheets produces small variations of the bending curve that have been utilised for the overlapping and interlocking of adjacent elements. This is the system of self-stabilisation of the vaults, and the intensity of the forces that need to be transferred into the ground along timber plates is kept to a minimum.

The exploration of the sheet material and the manipulation of its bending properties by controlling the number of layers of ply and the fibre direction of these layers was the beginning of the design process. The precise geometry of the bending curve emerged out of the distribution of matter, the hierarchy within plywood as the composite material and given load conditions. Based on a systematic investigation into the defining parameters, sheets of 18-millimetre (0.7-inch) thickness with fibres mainly in longitudinal directions have been used for the pavilion. The inscribed louvres within the sheets influence the bending curve by functioning as dead load, adding to the self-weight of the continuous strips along the edge of the sheets. Along these edge strips, two sheets of different lengths are overlaid and cross-braced by a sequence of cables that distribute all other load conditions evenly within the strips, and so reduce additional deformation of the arched form to a minimum.

The Bifurcated Bridge

The design proposal for a temporary bridge structure between two buildings at the AA in London was developed in collaboration with the Institute of Computational Design (ICD) at the University of Stuttgart. It is an exploration of the distribution of material with respect to the stress field within a given form. The design is based on a U-shaped component system built out of flat and single-curved prefabricated timber and plywood elements. The components are connected by means of two inlaid steel plates that enable the bridge to function as a 'simply supported' system that rests on the existing brick walls, with load transferred along the vertical faces of the components. The pedestrian surface is attached to the vertical faces by curved elements, and a small gap separates neighbouring components.

The overall arch-like form of the two legs of the bridge has been in part the result of a form-oriented design approach during the initial design phase, with Gaudí's hanging chain model as precedence. Due to the restraints of the support conditions, however, the bifurcating bridge cannot act as an arch; instead, the force flow is comparable to those within beams. In consequence, an uneven distribution of stresses occurs along the bridge. The subsequent refinements of the bridge design focused on the redistribution of material rather than on adaptation of the overall form.

As in the processes that govern the growth and development of bones, information from stress analysis was used within a feedback loop to successively relocate material along the U-shaped section of the components. This resulted in a differentiated distribution within the profile: a hollowing-out of the pedestrian surface, a thickening of the vertical load-bearing elements, and a concentration of material along the edge of the components. In addition, the process generated the formation of the curved top part of the U-shaped section; the integration of handrails as additional elements stiffened the bridge with respect to lateral loads.

below top, centre and opposite: The bridge connects three points of interest on three different levels: the reception area and central outdoor terrace with the main studio space.

bottom: Early prototype of a bridge component with even cross section. Components are tied together by steel cables, which later had to be replaced with steel plates due to the amount of sheer force within the vertical sections of the components.

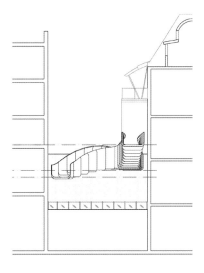

SOUTH ELEVATION

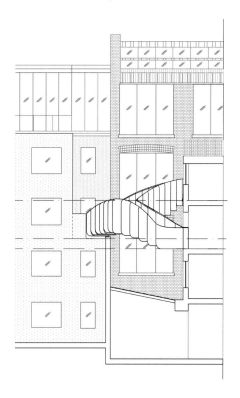

WEST ELEVATION

Both of the construction projects above show that material properties have the potential to unfold a generative logic of form-finding, a potential comparable to the use of geometric sets of rules within contemporary digital-design approaches.

Generative Material Logic

Both of the construction projects above show that material properties have the potential to unfold a generative logic of form-finding, a potential comparable to the use of geometric sets of rules within contemporary digital-design approaches. In this sense, materials have the inherent ability to 'compute' efficient forms, and to guide refinements as shown in the shaping of the components of the bridge. This material-immanent logic can support the fabrication and assembly, as in the pavilion project where no additional formwork was required in order to achieve the curved form. Using properties of the material world within the design process can help to simplify construction and make designs attainable. The incorporation of physical necessity of material behaviour as generative input, therefore, can help to unfold the freedom of design. Material constraints do not have to be understood as limitations to the design, but rather as sets of rules complementary to the geometric constraints defined by architectural intention. Form and material work hand in hand to process various load conditions; deformation of form and the distribution of material are reciprocal methods of design that help to 'digest' the flow of forces imposed upon the architecture. Freedom of design arises from the balancing of these two principles. ∆

Notes
1. For a review of the relationship between form and matter, see Katie Lloyd Thomas (ed), *Material Matters: Architecture and Material Practice*, Routledge (London), 2007.
2. The condition of having different structural and or dimensional properties along different axes.
3. The bony protuberances to which muscles are attached to the upper part of the femur.
4. Precedents to this field of work commence with the work of Alvar Aalto and Charles Eames in plywood, and the techniques of scoring, cutting and bending to achieve curvature have been established in a variety of materials in jewellery design, surface ornamentation, paper and other craft practices, as well as in airplanes and boats. Recent contributions include Skylar Tibbits' Surface Ornamentation at the Massachusetts Institute of Technology (MIT) (2008), and The Probotics by Knut Brunier, Anica Kochhar, Diego Rossel and Jose Sanchez of the Architectural Association Design Research Laboratory (AA DRL) (2010).

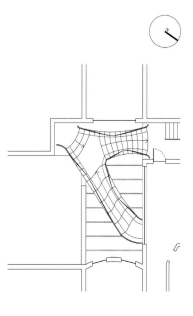

PLAN

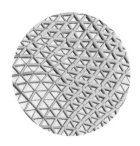

ENGINEERING INTEGRATION

REAL-TIME APPROACHES TO PERFORMATIVE COMPUTATIONAL DESIGN

Parametric techniques herald an age of predictive design. Results from simulations, analytical data and design performance criteria directly influence or drive architecture. However, this is still a relatively passive design approach: parameters go in, design comes out. **Al Fisher explains the work of Buro Happold's SMART Solutions team** on developing real-time simulations where the analysis is persistent within the model. Lightweight, mobile versions of tools traditionally reserved for detailed analysis can form the early conceptual stages of design. Interactive models can be tweaked and manipulated, with the live feedback of results providing a link to the materiality of the design. Through a responsive approach, hybrid design can be achieved that blends performance with design intent.

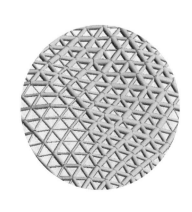

Hierarchical design matrix mapping the
sequential refinement of the design and
analysis process
Such an approach affords flexibility and
experimentation at the early stages through to
coordination and precision at construction.

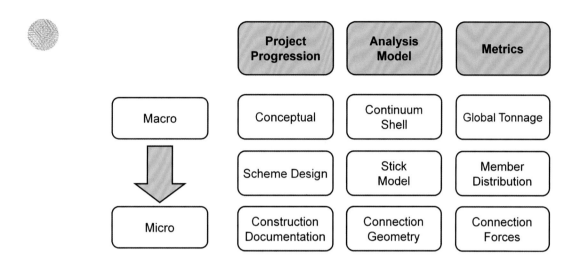

	Project Progression	Analysis Model	Metrics
Macro	Conceptual	Continuum Shell	Global Tonnage
	Scheme Design	Stick Model	Member Distribution
Micro	Construction Documentation	Connection Geometry	Connection Forces

The rapid development of parametric design tools, their ease of use and now continuing widespread adoption throughout the industry is transforming the way designs are created. A notable trend is the advancement of analysis and simulation tools. Increasingly, through exploiting the potential of engineering software, analytical data and design performance criteria can be used to influence or drive architecture. A full range of complex considerations can be simulated and accounted for in design. Specialist disciplines within engineering consultancy solve problems across a vast range of issues: the response to a bomb blast, crowd modelling, sand drift modelling, wind comfort, extreme vibration and environmental and sustainability ratings to highlight just a few. With this range of possible issues to account for, the designer is faced with new challenges.

In addition to the difficult, but previously more constrained question: How can criteria X be best met?, an increasingly important problem to be considered is: How can multiple design criteria be prioritised? With sophisticated computational capability enabling more design options to be considered, the skill is deciding how to tease out the pertinent criteria at the correct point in the design process. Powerful analytical

> Powerful analytical design tools can still prove to be impractical if they cannot influence and respond timely to the design. This goal can be achieved through two related aspects: firstly, careful control of the resolution and thus relevance of the data produced, and secondly, through effective communication of this information.

design tools can still prove to be impractical if they cannot influence and respond timely to the design. This goal can be achieved through two related aspects: firstly, careful control of the resolution and thus relevance of the data produced, and secondly, through effective communication of this information. It is in this area of conceptual analysis that there are currently high levels of research activity.

Conceptual Performance
To enable true performative-based design, performance criteria need to be fully integrated within the design development and thought processes during the early concept stages. It is at this point that experimentation is key. However, free experimentation, while maintaining detailed coordination across multiple specialist disciplines, can be seen as contradictory. It is therefore a challenge to explore concepts based on advanced simulation. Adopting a hierarchical approach to calculation as well as design is therefore essential. The depth of the modelling and accuracy levels should reflect the stage of design, with analysis during the early stages kept mobile, flexible and receptive to change.

The design matrix here illustrates this approach, where the level of design certainty, detail of analyses and the granularity of

Simulation of extreme non-linear behaviour
below: A snapshot of fluid structure interaction analysis shows propagation of a bomb blast shock wave and subsequent fracture and fragmentation of a facade.

Agent-based people-movement simulations
right: The simulations enable visualisation and clear communication of the emergent behaviour occurring as a result of the multiple potential design scenarios. SMART Move software enables strategic macro-masterplanning and crowd modelling down to detailed micro-simulation of individual rooms, queues and agents.

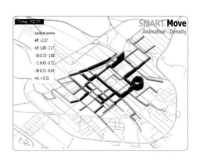

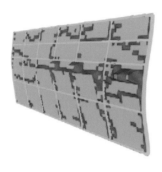

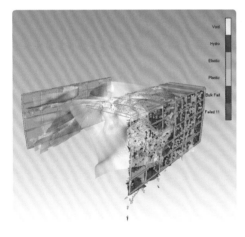

In complex projects, efficient collaboration across the various disciplines in the design team can be hindered by the glut of data that can be produced when dealing with multiple simulations, optimisations and design investigations.

their metrics are all progressively refined in parallel to the project development. The early experimental stages of design demand flexibility and thus starting from coarse, quick and disposable analysis models means the design team can respond rapidly to changes in concept. The example in the matrix is taken from the design of a free-form wide-span space frame structure. At the conceptual stages, the project is concerned with large quick assessments based on simple geometries and easily quantifiable results. As such, initial studies were performed, making approximation to a continuum shell and using high-level metrics such as global tonnage. When later coordination and increased accuracy is required, more detailed, rationalised and fully resolved models can be created. This approach ensures that information is relevant and meaningful and can be fed back into the design at all stages of the process, as well as minimising abortive work. In addition, developing tools as plug-ins to common commercial software such as Rhino3D, Autodesk Revit Architecture or Robot Structural Analysis enables this process to be formed integral to the design workflow.

Communication of Information

In complex projects, efficient collaboration across the various disciplines in the design

team can be hindered by the glut of data that can be produced when dealing with multiple simulations, optimisations and design investigations. Presenting raw analysis data in a rarefied form is therefore crucial to ensure influence over design decisions. For highly non-linear, chaotic or emergent problems, a simple single-value result or binary pass/fail outcome is often not possible, and mostly unhelpful for driving further design iterations. Computational fluid dynamics (CFD) is an obvious example where capturing the complexity of the spatial and temporal aspects of the problem is important. The intricacy of multidimensional information such as subtle perturbations and fluctuations can be observed and understood more readily in a dynamic visualisation of results.

People-flow modelling as a discipline provides an example of effectively analysing and communicating design data for complex non-linear and emergent scenarios. Here, hierarchical refinement and visualisation of analyses from macro-masterplanning models, involving simulations of hundreds of thousands of individual agents, down to microlevel modelling of congestion on a scale of individual corridors and rooms can be achieved. Examples of such scenarios modelled using SMART Move, Buro Happold's in-house agent-based people-flow modelling

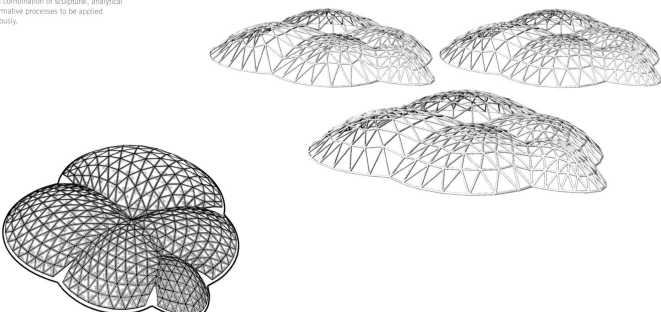

software, are illustrated here. The dynamic
visualisation of data greatly increases the
understanding of the scenario of interest and
helps communication to the rest of the design
team or fed direct to the client and other
project stakeholders.

The natural cross-pollination of
technologies across industries helps drive
these advancements in visualisation and
graphical representation. Historically,
methodologies for efficiently generating
and controlling free-form geometries were
developed by the automotive industry to
capture the sculptural forms of car bodywork.
More recently, techniques for efficient and
flexible modelling of arbitrary topology
surfaces have been adopted and developed
out of the computer animation and gaming
industries. In addition to computational
geometry, this convergence of computer-aided
design (CAD) and computer-aided engineering
(CAE) has seen analysis techniques being
adopted more widely as well. Numerical
discretisation approaches such as particle-
based modelling and the finite difference and
finite element methods have been adapted
for increased realism in visualisation. For
example, simplified, robust and, importantly,
stable versions of highly non-linear behaviour
such as fabric and fluid behaviour are now
routinely used for animation. Lightweight

forms of the notoriously complex Navier-
Stokes equations can now be solved in real
time for use in computer gaming. When
modelling scenarios purely for entertainment,
the emphasis is clearly on achieving a visually
convincing aesthetic over rigorously capturing
behaviour to a high degree of accuracy.
However, it is this blending of technologies
that can potentially enable more interactive
control of models.

Hybrid Performative Modelling
Controlling design processes based on
feedback from complex analyses can create
a highly constrained design space. When
considering the superposition of multiple
conflicting constraints and conditions,
concepts such as a single global optimum
become difficult to define, if not immaterial.
There is no single answer. As such an
analysis environment is required that enables
a trade-off to be made between soft and
hard constraints. An example of integrated
performative geometry is demonstrated here.

Approaches for defining and controlling
the generation of free-form geometry can be
subcategorised as analytical, performative
or purely sculptural. Finding a satisfactory
analytic or rule-based approach to describe
the multiple requirements of a highly
constrained programme can be challenging or

Andrew Wright Associates/S&P Architects with
Buro Happold, Scunthorpe Sports Academy,
Scunthorpe, North Lincolnshire, 2011
Close collaboration between the architects
and engineers enabled development of the
responsive form through novel form-finding and
optimisation techniques.

SMART Sizer
below and pages 112–113: Dynamic control of
non-linear structural optimisation enables global
behaviour to be understood and controlled.
Stiffness distributions can be manipulated
such that load paths can be sculpted through
structures.

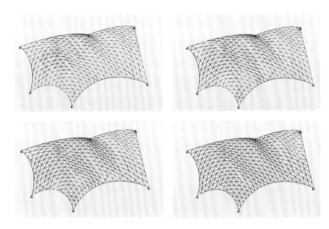

> With calculations persistent within
> the model, user interaction can
> occur in real time. Such an approach
> enables presentation of results in a
> form which the designer can usefully
> interact with and interrogate, and on
> which strategic design decisions can
> be based.

impossible. Equally, the control and precision
afforded through any singular design approach
may not lead to a solution.

These challenges were faced during the
early conceptual development of the form
and structural arrangement for Scunthorpe
Sports Academy (2011). Working closely
with architects Andrew Wright Associates,
initially analytical approaches to setting out
the structural centre line were explored. Due
to the inherently free-form nature of the roof
form, explicit rules and relationships could
not be defined where all criteria were fully
met to a satisfactory level. The multiple
design requirements to be satisfied included
structural performance, fabrication, aesthetics,
site constraints and cost, such that their
incompatible priorities led to no condition
governing. In parallel, physical modelling
processes were also explored. However,
no single approach could capture both the
complexity and flexibility required in the
control of the multiple design requirements.

A hybrid approach was therefore
developed allowing aspects from
different design approaches to be utilised
simultaneously. The setting up of parametric
models allows a distinction of 'hard' and
'soft' constraints of which soft parameters
can be dynamically controlled and the design
sensitivity explored. In addition, hybrid

design approaches allow constraints and
requirements to be combined and further
subcategorised as analytical, sculptural or
performative.

With calculations persistent within the
model, user interaction can occur in real
time. Such an approach enables presentation
of results in a form which the designer can
usefully interact with and interrogate, and
on which strategic design decisions can be
based. This establishes analysis as a true
design tool rather than simply forming the
production of results. The principle has been
taken further in the latest prototypes of Buro
Happold's SMART Form software. Here, the
designer can mould and interact directly with
analysis geometry and design properties. It is
this capability that computational approaches
can exploit, visualising and manipulating
abstract properties and characteristics,
processes impossible to perform on a physical
model, affording a deeper understanding of
model behaviour.

The screenshots of the firm's SMART
Sizer software illustrate interactive control
of structural optimisation parameters. The
potential dynamic modification of optimisation
criteria means that the designer can feel
the structural response and behaviour of
the design. In this case, by controlling the
global stiffness distribution throughout the

SMART Form
top: Real-time form-finding enables true performative-based design concepts to be explored.

Models embedded with analysis and persistent feedback
bottom: The models create tactility in computational design. The response can be felt by plucking at abstract properties such as elasticity or applying virtual forces to the model. Interactivity with these properties can lead to a deeper understanding of model behaviour and design sensitivity.

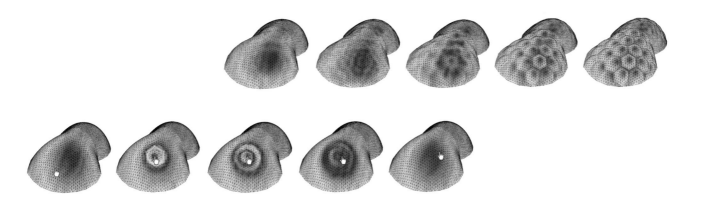

structure it can be designed to efficiently meet deflection and serviceability criteria.

Collaborative Design Modelling

Tools naturally impart their influence on design, both the process and the final product. Similarly, it is the design requirements that fuel the further development of tools. The evolution of technology initially replicates what we can already achieve through other, perhaps manual, processes, with more efficient methodologies, increasing productivity, increasing profitability, reducing time scales and simplifying workflow. However, a crucial outcome of development is the potential for genuine new capability.

The general movement, backed by government legislation, to adopt approaches to integrated modelling and building information modelling (BIM) platforms will see indisputable financial and process efficiency benefits. Efficiency in the end product also requires analysis and performance data to dovetail tightly within these processes. Interactive conceptual performance models potentially enable actual collaboration across analysis tools as well as the common repository for results. Centralised models enable allocation of user access to individual team members for relevant sections of a model. These concepts could be extended

to enable variable access and control of simulations, including variable resolution of models and data too. Intuitive, interactive conceptual tools will lead to greater collaboration as well.

With the availability of such tools and technology it is becoming increasingly easy to create intelligent models driven by control parameters. Interactive parametric modelling is creating a new design lexicon of poking, prodding and tweaking. This readiness and ubiquity in itself forms a challenge. Performative architecture will always only be achieved by the correct and timely identification of the pertinent design criteria. However, it is through tools that enable the softening of boundaries between analysis, design and sketching, and a more seamless transition between concept design, scheming and construction, that performative design intent can be realised. ⚙

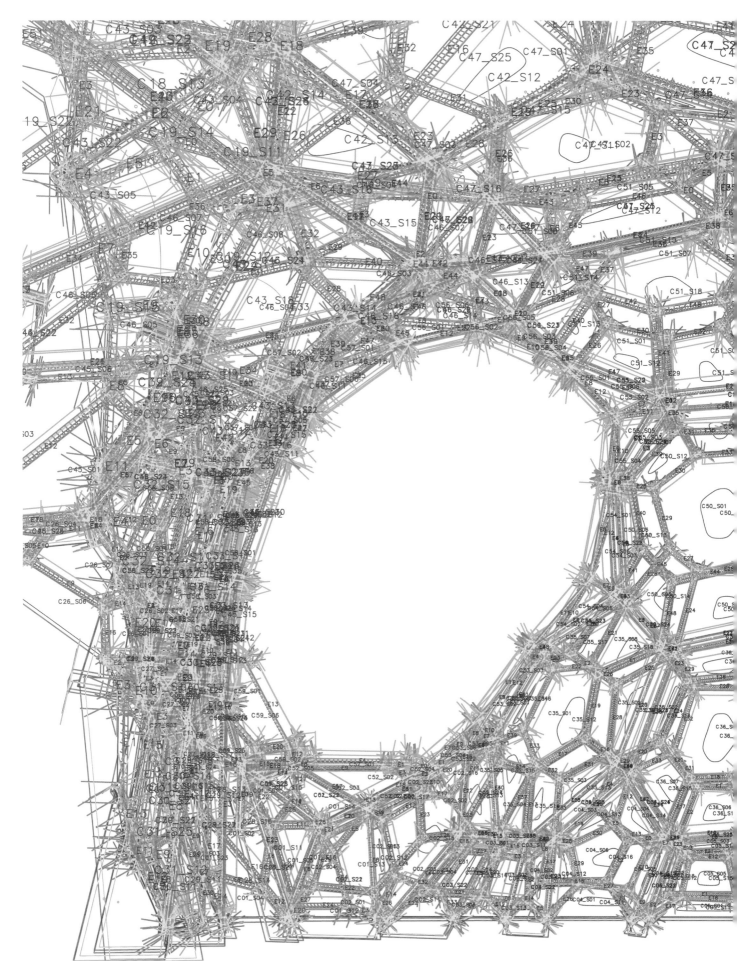

118

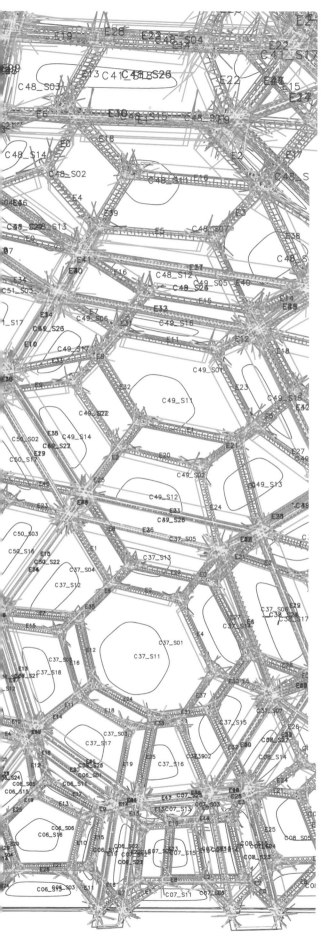

Achim Menges and Tobias Schwinn

MANUFACTURING RECIPROCITIES

Following in the footsteps of more progressive industries, digital fabrication in architecture is on the brink of shifting from task-specific computer numerically controlled (CNC) machines to more generic industrial robots. The change from machine hardware and control software developed to facilitate a specific fabrication process towards more open-ended and generic fabrication devices enables architects to design custom fabrication processes and machine-control protocols. **Achim Menges and Tobias Schwinn** present how these advanced machine capabilities expand the interface between design computation and physical materialisation.

Institute for Computational Design (Achim Menges) and Institute of Building Structures and Structural Design (Jan Knippers), ICD/ITKE Research Pavilion 2011, University of Stuttgart, Stuttgart, 2011
The encoding of parameters such as material thickness, density of finger joints based on local stresses, and angle between plates enables the automated generation of the tool path. The complete fabrication data incorporating parameters such as tool selection, rapid positioning, spindle speed and linear feed is embedded in the information model through automated computational routines.

In architecture, the multifaceted opportunities yielded by digital fabrication have been explored as CNC production has become more widely available in the building sector over the last 25 years.[1] However, until recently these explorations have been mainly focused on the use of CNC machinery specific to particular fabrication processes.[2] In parallel to these machines that are basically CNC progressions of long-established fabrication devices, another more generic type of digitally controlled machinery has been developed: the industrial robot. In the context of this technological evolution, the industrial six-plus axis robot represents the other end of the spectrum, as compared to CNC machinery highly specific to a given fabrication process. It is a completely generic and mostly undetermined fabrication system.

Generic Machines, Specific Control

Theoretically, the versatility of an industrial robot allows for a huge variety of fabrication processes to be implemented, as by design the robot is not predetermined to exclusively perform a specific task. But practically, this also means that out of the box, a robot cannot do very much of anything, and in its traditional usage scenario it will be manually 'taught' a sequence of manipulations such as the handling of crates in a warehouse or the welding of sheet metal on an assembly line. By and large, the accurate repetition of such a sequence is what the robot, aka industrial manipulator, has originally been designed for in its use in the automotive industry.

However, in the context of architectural prefabrication processes, the industrial robot represents the last link, or output device, in a digital chain of CAD-to-CAM data-processing steps that seamlessly link the final robotically manufactured artefact to a digital information model. This process is obviously not concerned with the indefinite repetition of a specific robotic manipulation; on the contrary, in contemporary practice it is mostly concerned with the ability to produce diversity. Therefore, in order to manufacture unique building elements, the numerical control of the robot has to be implemented through generative computational methods.

The robot, being at the intersection of the binary and discrete world of the computer and the material world in which architecture exists, represents the interface between design computation and physical materialisation. This opens up the opportunity not only to question the presumed unidirectionality of the flow of information from file to factory, but rather to investigate the possibilities for reversing or short-circuiting this flow by informing the digital design tools themselves with the procedural logic of fabrication and the physical characteristics of material systems.

Machinic Morphospace

Advances in the sophistication of CNC fabrication technologies, in particular in the area of machine hardware, and the shift towards more generic robotic machinery, create a potential for design applications that is largely untapped. In other words, if

The implementation of design principles derived from nature is proposed as a methodology to meaningfully populate the expanding design space that is offered by the machines.

a specific machinic configuration can be correlated to a space of possible producible outcomes, then this space appears to be unevenly populated. In evolutionary biology, the comparison of a population of individuals to the theoretical space that individuals can occupy is a key concept of morphological analysis. There, the term morphospace is used to describe concepts that see the morphological features of a specimen as actuations within a solution space or landscape of possible outcomes. The distinction between theoretical and empirical morphospaces provides a method to describe the actual morphology of, in this case, the development of a species as a subset of the virtually possible. This distinction is made in terms of scope: theoretical spaces are able to represent what is possible, or occupiable, and empirical spaces are renditions of what has actually been occupied.[3]

In the context of architectural fabrication, an extension of this concept can be applied as a reference frame relating the theoretical possibilities of fabrication parameters to their actual outcomes. As such, a specific morphospace is defined by its parameters, which in the case of the machines are their tools, materials, interfaces, degrees of freedom and so on. By consequence, the nature of different morphospaces is a function of their initial parameters. Theoretical morphospace is the space of possible outcomes, but it is also a fitness landscape; that is, not all areas can be meaningfully populated evenly. In this view, realised design projects are seen as individuals populating the empirical morphospace.

Actuation of Robotic Morphospace

The opportunities of contemporary CNC fabrication technologies have not only superseded the paradigms of serialisation and repetition that were predominant in 20th-century architecture; the relationship to the material itself, as the substrate that constitutes the man-made environment, has experienced a kind of sea change. Building materials are a finite and costly resource, a principle not unlike that by which biological systems in nature make use of their own resources. This notion is summarised in the recognition that in biology, material is expensive, but shape is cheap, whereas until today the opposite was true in the case of technology.[4]

The premise of the Performative Morphology project leading up to the ICD/ITKE Research Pavilion 2011, a collaborative research undertaking of the Institute for Computational Design (ICD) and the Institute of Building Structures and Structural Design (ITKE) at the University of Stuttgart,[5] is that, similar to nature, adaptation through geometric differentiation of building components in conjunction with novel methods of fabrication can yield performative modes of architectural production.[6] The focus of the project is on biomimetic design strategies in architecture, which form the basis of an investigation into integral material, structural and spatial systems. By the same token, it is also an example for the implementation of a specific design application on the generic robotic fabrication platform.

The implementation of design principles derived from

opposite bottom: The porosity of the inner layer not only reduces the overall weight of the structure, but also facilitates the assembly of the modules with detachable fixings. The size of the openings gradually reduces towards the single-layer region.

below: The project explores the architectural transfer of biological principles of the sea urchin's plate skeleton morphology through computational design and robotic manufacturing processes.

nature is proposed as a methodology to meaningfully populate the expanding design space that is offered by the machines. CNC machinery has the potential to facilitate the economical implementation of biology's mandate for adaptation of form and geometric differentiation. As opposed to merely translating biomorphic patterns from biology to architecture, the transfer of knowledge happens on a systemic and performative level, through the recognition of patterns in the way that problems are solved in biology and in engineering. Consequently, biomimetics is seen as a strategy for architectural and structural design. The goal is to implement a biologically informed material system that draws equally from design principles in nature and from those in fabrication.

Whereas most biological systems are characterised by material continuity between elements, there are a few natural systems based on discrete parts. These systems, most notably plate skeletons as those of sea urchins, offer interesting models for morphologically adaptable, robotically prefabricated building systems. Based on research on biological structures and in particular on the morphological analysis of the sand dollar species, which are part of the class of sea urchins (*Echinoidea*), a number of basic morphological design principles for plate structures have been identified from which a biologically informed material system is subsequently developed.

The shell of the sand dollar is composed of polygonal calcite plates that, through their specific topology, yield an extremely performative structural system where only normal and shear stresses occur along the joints. For example, unlike in many folded structures, here the morphology is always resolved with exactly three plates meeting at one point, which leads to the structural advantage that the plate joints are not, or are only marginally, exposed to moment forces. Furthermore, in sand dollars the articulation of the plate margins through rigid stereom projections allows for the interlocking of neighbouring plates.[7] Due to its particular structural behaviour, the sand dollar has been identified as a model for modular shell structures composed of prefabricated building elements. Similarly, finger joints, which in traditional woodworking connect force- and form-fitting elements through multiple interlocking teeth, have been identified as a fabricational equivalent of the sand dollar's stereom projections in that they are particularly suited to accommodate shear stresses. As an added benefit, finger joints allow for connections without any additional fastener and avoid warping effects during dimensional changes (for example, swelling or shrinking of wood) of the structural elements. Not only the sand dollar's global plate topology, but also its local constructional and functional morphology, informs the material system.

In addition to the local morphology of the sand dollar's plate skeleton, a number of biomimetic design principles have been established: heterogeneity, where the cell sizes adapt to local curvature and discontinuities; anisotropy, where cells are oriented according to the flow of structural stresses through the system; and hierarchy, where the cell configuration is composed of a

right: Echinoid morphology: sand dollars (echinoids belonging to the order *Clypeasteroida*) show a distinctive polygonal plate arrangement within their plate skeleton shell which constitutes one of the morphological principles for the computational design processes from which the research pavilion was derived. Schematic top view of a sea urchin (*Clypeaster*)

bottom: Stereom projections: microscopic view showing the stereom projections allowing for the interlocking of the calcite plates in sand dollar shells, which are particularly suited for accommodating shear stresses.

Markus Burger and Oliver Krieg, Robotically manufactured finger-joints system, Institute for Computational Design (ICD), University of Stuttgart, Stuttgart, 2010
below: The robotically manufactured finger-joint connection developed at the ICD allows for various types of plate topologies: two plates connecting at one edge, three plates meeting at one point and 3-D connections with six plates meeting at one point.

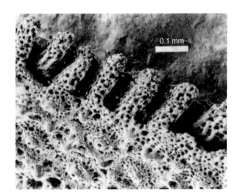

two-tier plate system that is meeting the requirements of the local morphology principle. At the level of the individual module representing the doubly curved plate of the sand dollar, the plates are joined through finger joints, always with three plates meeting at one point, allowing for a form- and force-fitting monomaterial connection.

By consequence, both structural design and the form-finding process that reflects these biomimetic design principles allowing for the generation of design variation through adaptation to changing system-external and system-internal constraints, have to be closely intertwined. Using finite element (FE) analysis, the structural behaviour of the system has been simulated and has continuously driven the evolution of the design; in parallel, the load-bearing capacity of physical prototypes has been tested and the results fed back into the simulation, which in turn informed the global topology of the system. Through this integrative computational design process based on the reciprocal effects of fabrication, form, structure, material and performance, the nominal material thickness could be minimised to just 6.5 millimetres (¼-inch) of cross-laminated plywood plates across almost all elements of the system. The structural capacity of the system allows the use of this extremely thin material, enclosing 200 cubic metres (7,063 cubic feet) of spatial volume using only 1.8 cubic metres (64 cubic feet) of wood.

The efficient fabrication of the more than 850 geometrically distinct building components, as well as more than 100,000 individual 3-D finger joints, necessitate the flexible and automated generation of the NC-Code on the basis of the digital information model. A closed digital information loop is a prerequisite for this process, including the design model, and structural analysis through to the numerical control of the robot. The automatically generated ISO-based NC-Code reflects the individual parameters of the seven-axis robotic fabrication process. Variables such as feed, spindle speed, down-cut and up-cut milling, as well as spatial orientation and rotation of the work piece on the turntable inform the NC-Code generation. Even the specific geometric constraints of the tool itself affect the global morphology in that certain geometric relations between plates are preferred over others. Ultimately, all of the plates are prefabricated on the university's seven-axis industrial robot, and then preassembled into cells of up to 26 individual plates. Following the mandatory weatherproofing, the robotically prefabricated cells are assembled on site.

Reciprocity

The industrial robot represents a platform on which a variety of different fabrication processes can be implemented. In this sense, the robotic fabrication of finger-joined plate structures represents an example for a design-to-product application that is compiled and hosted on this platform. This is akin to the ubiquitous apps that can be installed and run on a variety of 'hosts'. In the case of smartphones, the phone provides the generic platform on which a wealth of specific applications and usage scenarios can be implemented. In a similar

Institute for Computational Design (Achim Menges) and Institute of Building Structures and Structural Design (Jan Knippers), ICD/ITKE Research Pavilion 2011, University of Stuttgart, Stuttgart, 2011
The inherent material and milling constraints together with the geometry of the spindle describe a certain angle range that is one critical constituent for defining the machinic morphospace of the seven-axis robot for finger-joint production (top). The machine code is computationally generated relative to the individual working plane of each plate (bottom left). These tool paths are actuated through the inverse kinematics of the robotic arm (bottom right).

The individual plates with differentiated finger-joint connections are produced on a seven-axis industrial robot equipped with a custom-made combined cutting and milling tool. Each plate is robotically cut out of stock sheets of 6.5-millimetre (¼-inch) cross-laminated plywood, mounted on the turntable, robotically trimmed, cut and mitred according to the varying angles of the neighbouring plates.

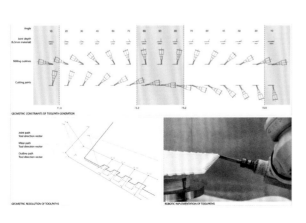

manner, microchips can be field programmed to encapsulate functionality that previously required a group of dedicated specific and monofunctional hardware components: an example is the software-defined radio which is implemented on field-programmable gate arrays.[8] The open-source Arduino platform represents the same principle. These microchips provide the hardware and the computational core of a system that is largely undetermined. The focus shifts from specific hardware to the specificity of the application that is hosted on these platforms.

This development away from specificity in hardware configuration to genericity and versatility can be understood as an undercurrent in the evolution of technology. Reciprocity emerges through the interaction of the user with the application and the exploitation of the platform's infrastructure for the purpose of a specific application. In the architectural context, reciprocity describes the relationship not only between the generic and the specific, between the hardware and the software or between the platform and the application; the discovery of reciprocity in the relationship between the actuated physical artefact and its virtual (digital fabrication) counterpart is the basis for the unlocking of the creative potential of CNC fabrication technologies and for meaningfully populating their expanding design space. ∆

Notes
1. Achim Menges, 'Manufacturing Diversity', ∆ Techniques and Technologies in Morphogenetic Design, Vol 76, No 2, 2006, pp 70–7.
2. Fabio Gramazio and Matthias Kohler, Digital Materiality in Architecture, Lars Müller Publishers (Baden), 2007.
3. Gunther J Eble, Developmental and Non-Developmental Morphospaces in Evolutionary Biology, Santa Fe Institute Working Paper 99-04-027, Santa Fe Institute, 1999.
4. Julian Vincent, 'Biomimetic Patterns in Architectural Design', ∆ Patterns of Architecture, Vol 79, No 6, 2009, pp 74–81.
5. ICD/ITKE Research Pavilion 2011: ICD (A Menges) and ITKE (J Knippers), M Gabler, R La Magna, S Reichert, T Schwinn, F Waimer, OD Krieg, B Mihaylov, P Brachat, B Busch, S Fahimian, C Gegenheimer, N Haberbosch, E Kästle, YS Kwon, H Zhai.
6. Oliver Krieg, Karola Dierichs, Steffen Reichert, Tobias Schwinn and Achim Menges, 'Performative Architectural Morphology: Robotically Manufactured Biomimetic Finger-Joined Plate Structures', Proceedings of the eCAADe Conference 2011, University of Ljubljana, Slovenia, 21–24 September 2011.
7. Adolf Seilacher, 'Constructional Morphology of Sand Dollars', Journal of Paleobiology, Vol 5 (3), 1979, pp 191–221.
8. Tobias Schwinn, 'Programmable Logic', in Neil Leach and Philip Yuan, Digital Futures, Tongji University Press (Shanghai), 2011.

The pavilion is assembled from more than 850 geometrically unique parts connected by more than 100,000 unique finger joints.

Close-up of finger-joint connection showing the biomimetic principle of three plates meeting at one point at the lower, first hierarchical level. On the upper, second hierarchical level, the computational process ensures that only three modules meet at one point.

This development away from specificity in hardware configuration to genericity and versatility can be understood as an undercurrent in the evolution of technology. Reciprocity emerges through the interaction of the user with the application and the exploitation of the platform's infrastructure for the purpose of a specific application.

The robotically prefabricated plates are assembled into modular building components. Due to the performance of the bionic morphology, all modules could be built from extremely thin sheets of plywood (6.5-millimetre/¼-inch).

Rupert Soar and David Andreen

THE ROLE OF ADDITIVE MANUFACTURING +

PHYSIOMIMETIC COMPUTATIONAL DESIGN FOR DIGITAL CONSTRUCTION

The recent adoption of the term additive manufacturing (AM) to describe a broad range of digital 'layer by layer' fabrication techniques comes 20 years since its inception and more than 10 years since architectural practices engaged with the technology for making prototypes and models. Soon this technology will join existing CNC subtractive and formative processes within the volume and mass-market sectors, where design complexity and increased functionality result in competitive advantage. It is also about a decade since researchers proposed additive manufacturing for construction. **Rupert Soar and David Andreen** introduce here the different construction-scale additive manufacturing systems currently in development. If linked to physiomimetic computational design strategies, these technologies provide novel possibilities for addressing architecture's manufacturing challenges in the face of energy expenditure, material resources and environmental impact.

Additive manufacturing (AM) has been largely adopted by the automotive, aerospace, military, medical and consumer goods sectors, initially as a method for producing prototype components, then for producing tooling and moulds and, most recently, for 'end-use' parts. This evolution reflects improved, selectively curable materials that have extended their performance to match standard engineering polymers and metal alloys. AM has penetrated high-value, short-run and 'custom' products due to increased complexity, design flexibility, material utilisation and increased functionality, compared to the traditional engineering processes of forming or machining components. It is no coincidence that layer-by-layer fabrication was adopted from traditional construction, yet we do not view traditional construction as generically 'additive'. This is because some aspects of construction are additive (building), some are formative (shuttering) and some are subtractive (centring), and, strangely, all three of these aspects can be found in any commercial AM machine. This observation is important, as really AM has nothing to teach construction about layer manufacturing per se, or its ability to form complex internal structures and assemblies within a form.

AM is about to transition to 'volume' or mass customisation. This requires new AM processes integrated into manufacturing cells alongside automated handling, assembly, subtractive and formative systems. This capability may have its greatest impact within mainstream volume construction where design integration (for example, monocoque structures), increased performance (dynamic building envelopes), 'design for disassembly' and 'product take-back' result in clear competitive advantage and global brand identity. This demands the integration of digital design, simulation, manufacturing and assembly as a continuum. Digital construction is ironically a 'digital vernacular'.

Research around additive manufacturing for construction (AM_C) can be traced to 1997, when Joseph Pegna demonstrated a method for the layer-by-layer selective curing and consolidation of cement structures by steam and posited its application for 'free-form fabrication' of construction components. However, it is worth noting the passing of a decade since the first attempts to realise AM_C. In 2001, Behrokh Khoshnevis at the Viterbi School of Engineering, University of Southern California, described and began assembling the materials and components for a large-scale combined extrusion and trowel 'automated construction' system called Contour Crafting. In 2003, exploratory work at Loughborough University focused on large-scale free-form fabrication to assess the feasibility of what was then called 'rapid manufacturing' for construction components, from which would emerge a large-scale (4 × 5 × 5 metre/13 × 16 × 16 foot) printing test bed. In 2004, Enrico Dini, then as

David Andreen, Duncan Berntsen, Petra Jenning and Rupert Soar, Agent Construction Cluster, SmartGeometry Conference, Copenhagen, 2011
previous spread: Investigation of design processes whereby multiple functions are simultaneously realised within a single structural solution. This emergent structure was realised over four days with volunteers acting as agents with conflicting objectives, such as openness, integrity, permeability, ventilation and connectivity, which must be constantly negotiated towards a solution. The work explores bottom-up negotiated solutions that will produce biological membrane capabilities for building envelopes.

Freeform Construction (Rupert Soar and Ian Wilkes), MineralStone, 2010
opposite: Additive manufacturing for construction places new demands on selectively curable materials which can satisfy technical, aesthetical and sustainability criteria. MineralStone is an inorganic mineral paste developed to suit a combined additive and subtractive process; it can be selectively triggered to harden into a stone-like machinable construction material.

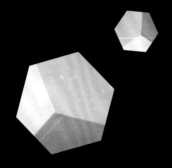

Dini Engineering based in Italy, patented and trialled a large-format epoxy resin and binder printing machine, and in 2007, inspired by the 3-D printing process, patented an inorganic large-format printing process called D-Shape and formed Monolite UK Ltd to commercialise the first AM_C demonstrator. In 2008, Richard Buswell from Loughborough University transformed the large-format printing capability into what is now called 'concrete printing'. The same year, Freeform Construction Ltd was formed to develop and commercialise the MineralJet process.

Progress has been steady, if not sporadic. The concept of AM_C has been driven, encouraged and fostered by many creative minds within architecture who see an output technology to materialise exponentially complex forms. Architecture is rapidly progressing through an era of parametricism to one of morphology, or physiomimetic design. However, the next significant development in AM_C is overdue. As AM enters mass-market manufacturing, it will probably first undertake customised operations producing elements that are geometrically close to the final part ('near net shape'), combined with conventional 'near net shape' formative operations and linked to digital or CNC subtractive ('net shape') operations as a process continuum. Are the drivers the same for the construction sector? Will the investment opportunities mimic the year-on-year growth seen in the evolution of what was once called a rapid prototyping technology to what is about to become mainstream additive manufacturing?

A Point of Convergence

It is a time for a reassessment of AM_C by architectural engineers and the broader construction community. We are some way from on-site AM_C, but this does not exclude 'near site'. However, what is certain is that AM_C will first emerge as an off-site capability. Like the adoption of AM into manufacturing, AM_C will first address niche markets, but potentially have greater impact within volume markets. For AM_C to enter 'volume' construction, it must form part of an integrated, digitally driven additive, digital subtractive and digital formative continuum. It must realise greater performance than free-form aesthetics alone. It will enable design freedom combined with greater function, and it must address sustainability head-on. For this to happen, three components must converge. These are new, selectively curable phase-change materials, new processes at construction scales, and new design capabilities from which new product capabilities and applications will emerge.

New Materials

The first commercial, selective phase-change materials for AM_C are 'aggregate/binder' and paste systems. Two examples are D-Shape's magnesium oxide aggregate and binder system and Freeform Construction's high-density calcium sulphate paste called MineralStone. Unlike concrete, these do not set when mixed with water, but have a chemical 'trigger' which selectively activates crystallisation and solidification. Both materials break the cost model used by many AM technology producers; the cost of the machine is offset by the cost of the material supplied, which is typically $100 per kilogram. This model cannot work at construction scales: selectively curable phase-change materials for construction applications must come in at $100 per tonne.

AM_C materials must address the future, they must be synthesised from by-product sources, be indigenous to the location where they are transformed into products, and be fully recyclable within both the factory environment and at the end of the product's life. This latter requirement could be an entry point for AM_C products and components 'designed for disassembly'. Selective activation must induce crystallisation, but not instantaneously. At the scale of partitions, panellisation and cladding systems, crystallisation should take place over minutes, not seconds, to reduce exothermic heat, which can be cumulative at these scales.

Where D-Shape's and Freeform Construction's materials may differ is in their application. D-Shape's material is a concrete substitute immediately suited to external, load-bearing and monocoque applications, and Freeform Construction's material is for non-load-bearing internal applications where high-tolerance and high-density (polished) finishes are required. However, there could be greater benefit in integrating these materials in a single monocoque solution, ie structure and finish. Both companies have developed their materials for near net shape additive fabrication, but Freeform Construction is deliberately linking an additive near net shape capability to a subtractive net shape detailing operation in one process.

New Processes

Contour Crafting tackled one of the first issues of fabrication at construction scales: how to deposit bulk quantities of material (with a centimetre-scale nozzle) to keep the build times down, while resolving micron-scale detail required for the finish. It simultaneously extrudes at the macroscale, then shapes at the microscale. It can work at more than two scales of resolution within any single deposited layer; by 'extrude trowelling' rapid curing walls or a 'skin build', the space inside the part can be backfilled with a generic concrete. This points to a departure from conventional construction methods that begin assembly at the metre scale and proceed downwards, with each subsequent operation, down to the micron scale with the polished finishes on surfaces. This cannot be carried out in a single operation, so components representing each scale of the structure are assembled a piece at a time. To overcome the

Behrokh Khoshnevis, Contour Crafting, Viterbi School of Engineering, University of Southern California, Los Angeles, 2011
Contour Crafting was the first AM_C initiative to construct a large-scale additive machine for the construction industry. Through concrete extrusion and shaping by a gantry-mounted robotic system, it envisions rapid on-site construction combining robotic 'dry' assembly of components with robotic 'wet' extrusion of structures for the housing sector.

Enrico Dini (Monolite UK Ltd), D-Shape, 2007
The D-shape process selectively solidifies stone powder through chemical activation, producing very large, self-supporting structures due to the presence of the unbonded aggregate that supports complex parts during the build. D-Shape is the first large-format process where complex internal geometry can be incorporated into the build.

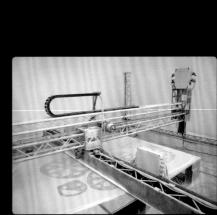

inevitable discrepancies and 'tolerance drift' when assembling an estimated 3,000 components in a typical house, construction is as much about designing interfaces, seals and gaskets as it is about the physical production of the form.

AM currently fills the niche for objects from approximately 1 cubic millimetre (0.00006 cubic inches) up to 1 cubic metre (35 cubic feet). Layer fabrication techniques, however, extend well into the micrometre (printed circuits) and increasingly the nanometre scale (silicon chips). Likewise, above the scale of 'things you can see or hold', there will not be one single or 'mega' scale, but many 'niche scales'. Contour Crafting could exploit 'on site' at scales covering rooms to buildings. D-Shape could exploit 'near site' at scales covering pods to rooms. Concrete Printing could exploit 'on site' for foundations and primary structures, and Freeform Construction's proposed MineralJet exploits 'niche scales' above 1 cubic metre (35 cubic feet) up to pods, partitioning, cladding and panellisation.

The concept of testable prototypes of a structure is relatively new, and is satisfied largely by simulation and visualisation software. However, architects, when communicating with their clients, need detailed model-making capabilities above 1 cubic metre (35 cubic feet), for 1:50 up to 1:500, and urban planners need detailed models at 1:1000. These models typically require builds greater than 1 cubic metre (35 cubic feet), but detail at less than 1 cubic millimetre (0.00006 cubic feet), which could be achieved by combining additive and subtractive methods into a single process. Architectural engineers are discussing the value of structural and detailing prototypes for models at 1:5 to 1:1 scales – (within build volumes of 3 to 5 cubic metres (106 to 176 cubic feet) – for interface design or wind tunnel testing, and these too require smooth micron-scale finishes that only a subtractive process can deliver.

Freeform Construction's solution is an interchangeable deposition head that is swapped with a cutting-tool head during the build. They are not pursuing a predefined articulated robot or gantry-type placement device. Gantry robots are easy to assemble and cheap to run, but the build envelope is commonly restrained within a frame. Inversely, articulated robots are expensive to run, but are not tied to movements within a building envelope. An articulated robot with an additive deposition and/or subtractive fabrication head can work inside pods, build artefacts of a greater size than itself, and move fabricated parts and components around a factory as part of a sequence of operations. This becomes relevant for cladding and panellisation systems, for example.

To fabricate a set of custom high-performance panels, as part of a secondary cladding retrofit, digital scan data of the building is captured on site and a digitally generated functional skin created to enhance U-value, acoustic and service utility criteria

Richard Buswell, Sungwoo Lim, Tony Thorpe, Alistair Gibb and Simon Austin, Concrete Printing, Innovative Manufacturing and Construction Research Centre, Loughborough University, Loughborough, 2008
The project explores novel high-build cement paste systems with 'off-the-shelf' construction technologies such as concrete spraying tied to gantry systems and computer control. The process developed at Loughborough uses a cement-based mortar that is extruded from a print-head mounted on a three-axis gantry.

Freeform Construction, MineralJet, 2010
The proposed MineralJet technology combines 'near net shape' additive fabrication and net shape subtractive machining for construction models and building components, where high accuracy, connectivity of parts and integration within a production cell are important.

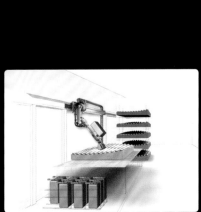

while satisfying window and door detailing and so on. The digital skin is then sectioned (at 2 × 3 metres/6.5 × 9.8 feet for handling) into approximately 50 custom cladding panels. The panels may be between 100 and 400 millimetres (3.9 and 15.7 inches) thick, depending on the performance criteria, and must be fabricated at 3 to 5 millimetre (0.1 to 0.2 inch) resolution within a day, as part of a 24-hour unmanned operation. Panels have a void-to-solid ratio of around 80:20, which is nearly one panel every 30 minutes and approximately 20 litres (4.4 gallons) of build paste. They must be printed, textured/finished (meaning external face texturing and building interface detailing to match the existing building profile), cured, and have the interface profiles machined on to each panel edge, before batching and transport at less than £250 per panel.

New Design Tools

Digital design to manufacturing begins with digitising of the input parameters. This may include the physical scan of an existing building, the continuous scanning of the construction process on site, and could extend to measures of physical properties, such as moisture permeability, thermal flux or usage and behavioural data. This data must be processed through algorithmic design tools and traditional design processes to deliver solutions that fulfil specified performance criteria, whether stylistic, programmatic, environmental or functional. In

this context, AM_C is not actually an end stage, but part of a continuum of inputs and outputs feeding to and from each other, resulting in the complete documentation of a structure's performance (through algorithms) 'as built', which implies that, like AM_C (digital outputs), 3-D scanning (digital inputs) needs to be fully integrated into the manufacturing process. This overturns linear 'design and build' processes and replaces them with a continuous loop existing in both physical and virtual space from which modifications and adaptations to existing designs can be generated through the building's life.

By removing the bottleneck between digital design and fabrication, both detail and non-standardisation emerge which may well be classed as a 'digital vernacular'. Emerging design methodologies challenge standardisation. NURBS modelling, optimisation, scripting and simulation often lose their logic when taken through realisation stages. AM_C provides the means to undo this conflict as it removes the manufacturing constraints on customisation and complexity. This is not a complete departure from standardisation, but, rather, a shift from physical, component-based standardisation to a virtual standardisation that places completely new demands on both the execution and regulation of the industry. In this new environment we are forced to remodel the relationship between the plan and the object. These are no longer separate. Designing at the process level of a building and its occupants –

Freeform Construction
(David Andreen and Petra Jenning)
MineralSkin
2010

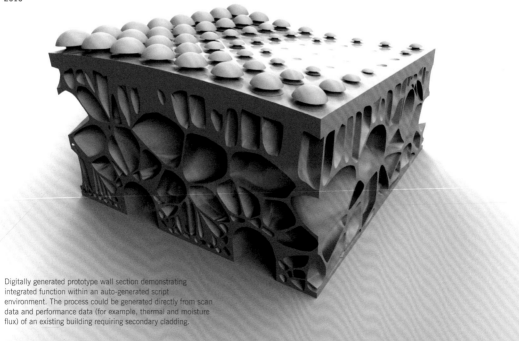

Digitally generated prototype wall section demonstrating integrated function within an auto-generated script environment. The process could be generated directly from scan data and performance data (for example, thermal and moisture flux) of an existing building requiring secondary cladding.

how it works as opposed to a description of what it does (its function) and how it looks (its form) – implies design of a structure that delivers physiological needs such as hydration, light, security, information and warmth/coolth, and creates the potential gradients required to deliver them to the occupants.

Physiomimetic computational design (PCD) operates on this algorithmic process level. PCD links the form-finding relationships in a script directly to a materialisation process, where agents interrogate a process database (for example, movement of gas, waste, light, access, even aesthetics) to identify a set of optimal materials from which a single structure that meets all these process requirements can be fabricated. The output data from the materialisation process links directly to the inputs or variables in the script, which contains the spatial relationships for each material and the processes it represents. PCD overcomes the problem of trying to miniaturise separate process components within less space by folding the process components and sharing the material capabilities across multiple functions. It produces structures that literally squeeze more functions into less form and can be output directly to AM or AM_c. PCD is not inspired by, nor mimics, either the forms or functions in nature. It mimics matter folding and process component integration as a natural outcome of agents negotiating for materialisation, which *is* nature.

Moving Forward

Though AM technologies emerged within mechanical engineering, their adoption took them far wider into aerospace, military, medical and leisure markets, to name just a few. AM has moved from a prototyping capability, with year-on-year growth for 20 years, to a niche high-value 'end-user' customisation tool, and is about to integrate within mainstream volume manufacturing. Interest in AM by the construction sector has been sporadic, partly because of the disconnect between design and construction, but mostly as there is an issue of scale. A model-making capability is fine for an architectural practice, but cannot be applied to the 1:1 of building components. However, the expectation of AM's imminent engagement with volume markets is triggering progressive construction companies to look again at the technology and ask what gains can be had.

Commercial AM_c processes will initially address high-value markets, with products of capitalisable complexity, but will readily penetrate volume off-site markets by 'breaking the model', where off-site construction companies feel they must match the look of traditionally built on-site buildings. Build it free-form and customer expectations rise, and the competition with traditional on-site construction evaporates. Some global construction companies are already aware that, like cars and consumer goods, design and engineering are integral to innovative manufacturing.

Digital design to manufacturing begins with digitising of the input parameters. This may include the physical scan of an existing building, the continuous scanning of the construction process on site, and could extend to measures of physical properties, such as moisture permeability, thermal flux or usage and behavioural data. This data must be processed through algorithmic design tools and traditional design processes to deliver solutions that fulfil specified performance criteria, whether stylistic, programmatic, environmental or functional.

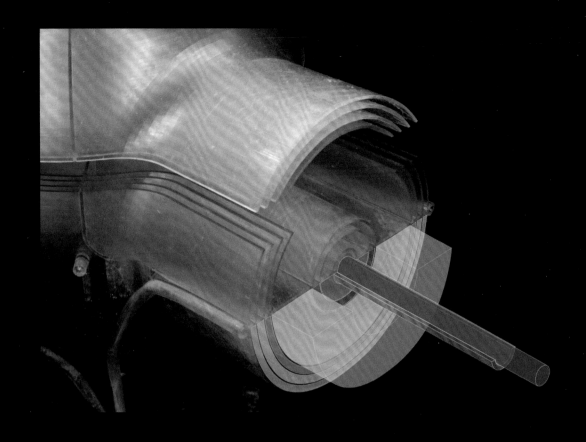

The first AM$_C$ products to enter the market may well be less spectacular than some of the visions, but no less significant.

Between the two institutional (University of Southern California and Loughborough University) and two fledgling commercial groups (Freeform Construction and Monolite) in Europe and the US that have engaged with this task, much ground has been covered over the last decade. Each has taken a unique approach based largely on issues of scale, resolution and cost. Each has developed new and novel, selectively curable phase-change materials, which either reflect current material resources or look forward to address the pressures of sustainability, recycling, 'design for disassembly' and 'product take-back'. Each has produced novel process solutions, each selecting niche scales, niche deposition solutions and niche resolutions, which, when considered as a whole, greatly mitigate the entry-point decisions many in the construction industry will be making over the next few years. The first AM_C products to enter the market may well be less spectacular than some of the visions, but no less significant. ⌂

Rupert Soar, Integrated Utility Node, FP7 I3Con project, Loughborough University, 2008 and Smart Geometry Conference, Barcelona, 2010
Integrated service utility node concept showing how scripts can be driven by function. HVAC and ME processes are integrated within a single system. The solution explores space saving by: 1) the proximity of the 'process space' for each service; 2) the sharing of materials across multiple services and functions; and 3) outputting an exoshell structure to the stereo-lithography apparatus (SLA). Low-melt alloys and flexible polymers were injected within the interstitial spaces separating each process. The injected metal alloys and polymer form contiguous shells within the structure to satisfy multiple functions simultaneously: metal for strength, shielding and conduction, and polymers for sealing, insulation and ductility within a single structure.

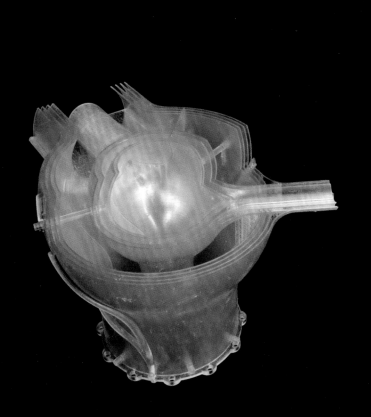

Bob Sheil

DISTINGUISHING BETWEEN THE DRAWN AND THE MADE

COUNTERPOINT
02/2012
№ 216
△D

Here **Bob Sheil**, Director of Technology and Computing at the Bartlett School of Architecture and co-organiser of the 2011 Fabricate Conference at UCL, pulls back on the rush towards material computation. With the blurring of the projected image and the constructed artefact, there is the very real danger of reducing 'architectural production to a systematic industrial exercise'. This fails to recognise the extent to which ideas and performance are transformed, developed and refined through the very process of making.

*One of the greatest challenges
has been to transcend the limited
possibilities of these tools*

While we can see how computation in architecture has developed an array of powerful tools for the development and evolution of geometric complexity, crossing the material threshold raises significant questions regarding the objective of design information, the status of the built work being generated, and the difference between simulation and fabrication.

Prior to the adoption of computer-aided design (CAD), architectural drawings were made using cumbersome tools that had not changed in any radical sense for more than 2,000 years. The compass, ruler, divider, protractor, callipers and square were in the possession of Egyptian, Chinese and Roman draughtsmen long before their Renaissance descendants. Other than the evolution of more precise instruments and more stable materials on which to draw, the standard tool set of the architectural designer remained remarkably consistent until the late 20th century. For the architect who has wished to break from tradition, one of the greatest challenges has been to transcend the limited possibilities of these tools and understand the difference between architectural propositions that are possible to make but difficult to draw, or possible to draw and difficult to make.

Lurking within this equation was a design intent that existed between the drawing and the artefact, one that relied upon conversation with other disciplines, trades and experts to be fulfilled as a physical entity. Implicit information on the specific production tools that might be used to make the design, or how such tools should be used, maintained, deployed or controlled, was limited. Only in instances such as the profile of mortar joints in brickwork, for example, might visual information and the technique of how the desired profile be struck become synthesised. If not implied in this way, or noted in specification clauses, decisions on production tooling were placed in the domain of the fabrication process which took responsibility for selection of appropriate tooling, standards, craft, durability, use, appropriateness of specific material samples, finish, delivery, and so on. In this context, it was understood that the architectural drawing as an instruction to make was highly constrained and limited, and that its primary focus was to define and secure the required outcome while allowing essential room for negotiation on how this was achieved. For the architectural design to be made, other drawings, such as shop drawings, were required as a rehearsal to making.

Peter Webb, Terra Therma, Diploma Unit 23, Bartlett School of
Architecture, UCL, 2009–10
left: Ideas and materials are metaphorically and literally
extrapolated from a site in North London and developed as
prototypical building components for a space of variable
temperature and humidity. The elements are extruded through a
digitally controlled variable jig.

Phil Ayres, Digital Material, from the Persistent Model project,
2010
right: The Persistent Model proposes a shift from the familiar
and established linear progression from representation to
artefact. A circular relationship permits the artefact to re-inform
the representation after disturbance from the environment.
Representation and artefact coexist – the ideal feeds into the actual,
and the actual feeds back to the ideal, tempering and steering its
predictive nature. Control is passed and shared.

The nature of this exchange has been significantly altered
by CAD/CAM, the fusion of drawing and manufacturing
technologies that plug design information with the production
equipment that makes what is described. Despite the many
advanced levels of capability this technology provides, its
potential to release design constraint, open new frontiers,
and extrapolate results not previously achievable has the
potential to bypass many of the essential transactions between
design and making that are incorporated in the exchange
between either field of expertise. Thus not only has the
architectural drawing altered its role as a carrier of design
information, so too has the architectural model, the prototype
and the speculative construct. The neat divisions that once
commissioned, sequenced and qualified these key productions
are converging, and the degree of cross-fertilisation between
each mode of representation provided by digital tooling
has generated a turbulent network of information flux. It is
within this context that we must examine implications for the
production of architecture that are posed in this issue of $\triangle$.

The transposition of the performance of physical materials
into a computational realm that subsequently decants what
is explored back into a physical realm is a sequence of
challenging translations. In the first instance it seeks to identify
a direct relationship between the performance of digital and
physical matter, and secondly it seeks to interpret highly
complex, dynamic and living systems as a template for form-
generation. Quite apart from the inevitable selectivity involved,
such an approach has the potential to reduce architectural
production to a systematic industrial exercise devoid of the
immeasurable and immaterial qualities that make it more
than the sum of its parts. It is the manner in which design
information allows for indeterminacy and anticipates the
possibility of how it can be made that make it work in the form
of a built artefact. The skill in describing architecture before it
is built is to make design information that anticipates, rather
than dictates, how it is translated through time, site, materials,
fabrication processes, assembly and use, and to understand
the difference between the first prototype and the last. Without
such a critical allowance, the built artefact is no more than
a physical render of a projected image where the exploration
of its performance as a construct ceased at the point of
simulation.

Constraints of any kind have long frustrated designers,
but now, as formal limitations subside and the array of what
is possible to describe through information escalates, the
question of what informs the making of architecture has
become increasing ambiguous. Much of what is promoted as
architectural invention through the power of digital processing
has emphasised how design information for more complex
architectural forms is supplied, but not how the subsequent
artefact is made. Key to ensuring that these concerns lead
to measured decisions is the need to remain aware of the

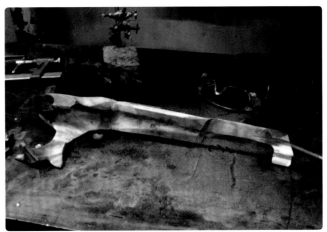

difference as well as the similarity between drawn and made things, particularly where linkages are being made on things that grow. So how are we to read the constructs of material computation? Should they be tested against the architectural criteria of firmness, commodity and delight, or are they a form of beta architecture that warrants an alternative judgement?

Through digital manufacturing processes, ideas that might have remained as an experimental *esquisse* in a previous age are being manifested in physical form. They are prototypes of a particular kind; constructs seeking to validate potential that has emerged through computational investigation, deliberate tests that are seeking to narrow the distance between the digital and the material. Among the repertoire of such emerging productions, it may be argued that a new breed of design artefact has arrived in the form of research concept proofs. When we consider this typology within a technical context, we might think of 1:1 facade assemblies tested for water tightness or sound absorption. We might think of structural elements tested for their load-bearing strength or stiffness, or we might think of material assemblies tested for their performance under impact, daylight, humidity, and so on. However, when the construct is presented as design evidence, the relationship between design information and built artefact is under scrutiny.

For the design team, the as-built work clearly provides some feedback on how it operates as a physical construct

Through digital manufacturing processes, ideas that might have remained as an experimental esquisse *in a previous age are being manifested in physical form. They are prototypes of a particular kind; constructs seeking to validate potential that has emerged through computational investigation*

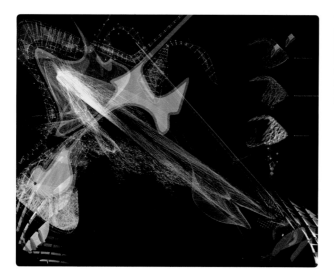

Emma-Kate Matthews, Spaces of Uncertainty – The Augmented Instrumentalist, Diploma Unit 23, Bartlett School of Architecture, UCL, 2010–11
below (all) and page 136 (right): Composite model, acoustic simulation, and sound perspective of a small listening chamber for a proposed performance space on the Venice Moses Barrier. Design as a hybrid of formal representation, manufacturing data, sound clips and environmental simulation.

As a construct of minimal programmatic requirement, it provides a convenient stage on which to present the underlying arguments that reside solely in the design enquiry, but not elsewhere.

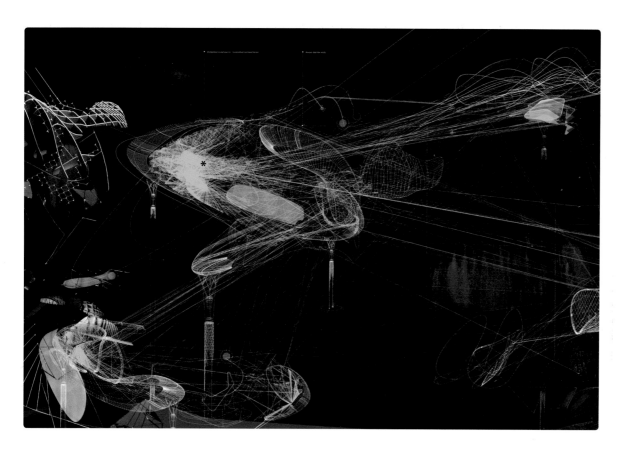

Matt Shaw/ScanLAB Projects, Subverting the
Lidar Landscape, Diploma Unit 23, Bartlett
School of Architecture, University College
London (UCL), 2008–09
below: Point-cloud image of a speculative
building component captured from a 3-D laser
scanner. Material defects and unseen anomalies
are detected by the scanner and appear in the
point cloud as digital noise. We have yet to fully
understand the behaviour of real materials in
digital space.

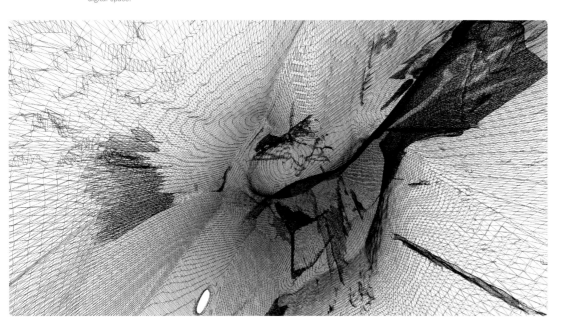

where the act of assembly and erection is as important as the finished result. Attention is directed to qualities of surface, structure, materiality, fabrication and form. The point that seems to be in focus, however, is how closely the built work resembles its digital master, and not how the ideas were transformed through making. What is presented in built form, therefore, is an attempt to validate the design enquiry by escaping the exclusivity of paper architecture. Yet the pavilion as the adopted typology for many of these investigations is a problematic model. As a construct of minimal programmatic requirement, it provides a convenient stage on which to present the underlying arguments that reside solely in the design enquiry, but not elsewhere. When these enquiries are pinned on rules for dynamic and evolutionary spatial propositions, of great importance is how the resulting artefact represents such exuberance in its physical form. If it does not, a peculiar contradiction ensues, which is further deepened when it is not clear why the particular iteration that was built was selected from the spectra of others. Where this occurs, and in comparison to the underlying genesis of growth, the pavilion is reduced to an architecture of rigor mortis, an object of ambiguous architectural status.

For these enquiries to go further, and be shared as valuable alternatives to shaping the built environment, more robust interrogation and critique of the built results are required. How different are they to the digital model? Are they behaving as predicted? And has the process of their manufacture delivered a result that tells us more about the research than a fully described digital model? If these questions are not addressed, this is a reality of a very exclusive kind; a beta-reality that is stage-managed to demonstrate specific challenges in digital processing or material manipulation that exist as simulations, rather than address the role such enquiries might take up in wider architectural realms such as occupancy, purpose, duration, environmental conditions, adaptability and context. Where it is implied that materials are synthesised as physical and digital matter, it is important to remember that built architecture is not made of points, vectors, splines and algorithms, but of stuff that has a habit of misbehaving unexpectedly, and of space that is defined through far greater complexities than its outer form. ⌂

Sean Ahlquist is a research associate and PhD candidate at the Institute for Computational Design (ICD) at the University of Stuttgart, where he is teaching and developing research in the field of computational design, heuristics and material behaviour for form-active structures. He has taught at the University of California Berkeley and California College of the Arts, and founded the design firm Proces2. He holds a master of architecture degree from the Emergent Technologies and Design (EmTech) programme at the Architectural Association (AA) in London.

David Andreen is a doctoral candidate and research engineer at University College London (UCL). His research area is in architecture and physiomimetics – the deep integration of physiological processes in the built environment – through computation and digital manufacturing.

Philip Ball is a freelance science writer, and previously an editor for *Nature*. He has published many books and articles on all areas of the natural sciences and their interactions with art and the wider culture, including the trilogy *Nature's Patterns: Shapes, Flow, Branches* (Oxford University Press, 2009).

Cristiano Ceccato is an associate at Zaha Hadid Architects. His professional focus includes design and development of building infrastructure and cladding, geometric and computational rationalisation and constructability resolution, project governance, cost control and construction supervision. He previously worked for Frank O Gehry in Los Angeles and was also a co-founder of Gehry Technologies, where he worked on a wide range of projects and interdisciplinary research with Boeing. He trained as both an architect and computer scientist, and has practised and taught architecture in Europe, Asia and the US. He received degrees from the AA and Imperial College in London, and is a Fellow of the Royal Society of Arts.

Karola Dierichs is an architect and doctoral candidate at the ICD at the University of Stuttgart. Her research focuses on aggregate architecture and the related processes of machine and material computation. She was educated at the TU Braunschweig, the ETH Zurich and the AA in London, from which she graduated from the EmTech programme with a distinction. She has taught at both the AA in London and the University of Stuttgart, and her work has been exhibited at a number of institutions including the International Architecture Biennale Rotterdam (IABR).

Al Fisher leads the complex geometry discipline within Buro Happold's SMART Solutions team. His research focuses on the definition, generation and manipulation of complex architectural geometry, in particular performative-based design where the engineering requirements and the architecture are inextricably linked. While at Buro Happold he has developed approaches to form-finding, rationalisation and optimisation for projects including timber grid-shells, tall buildings and sports stadia. He previously studied for his masters and PhD in civil and architectural engineering at the University of Bath.

Moritz Fleischmann is a former research associate and PhD candidate at the ICD at the University of Stuttgart. His research focuses on the use of physics-based modelling in early stages of the architectural design process. He has taught seminars and design studios at the TU Munich and the University of Stuttgart. He holds a diploma of architecture (Dipl-Ing.) from the RWTH Aachen and a master of architecture degree from the EmTech programme at the AA in London.

Jan Knippers received his PhD in structural engineering from the University of Berlin. Since 2000 he has been the head of the Institute of Building Structures and Structural Design (ITKE) at the University of Stuttgart, and since 2001 a partner at Knippers Helbig Advanced Engineering with offices in Stuttgart and New York.

Toni Kotnik is an assistant professor at the Institute for Experimental Architecture at the University of Innsbruck, and a senior researcher at the Chair of Structural Design at the ETH Zurich. He studied architecture and mathematics at ETH Zurich, the University of Tübingen, and the University of Utah, and received his doctoral degree from the University of Zurich. His practice and research work has been published internationally and is centred on the integration of scientific knowledge into the design process with a focus on the relationship between digital architectural design, geometry and material behaviour.

Julian Lienhard graduated in civil engineering from the University of Stuttgart. He is currently working towards his PhD at the same university's ITKE, which has its research focus on fibre-reinforced materials and bio-inspired elastic structures.

Ferdinand Ludwig is an architect and assistant professor at the Institute of Theory of Architecture and Design (IGMA) at the University of Stuttgart, where he coordinates the Baubotanik research group. He is currently working on his PhD thesis 'Horticultural construction techniques and botanically based design rules'. The Baubotanik research group is supported by Deutsche Bundesstiftung Umwelt (DBU).

Neri Oxman is an architect and designer, and is the Sony Corporation Career Development Professor and Assistant Professor of Media Arts and Sciences at the MIT Media Lab where she directs the Mediated Matter research group. Her group explores how digital design and fabrication technologies mediate between matter and environment to radically transform the design and construction of objects, buildings and systems. She received her PhD in design computation as a Presidential Fellow from MIT, where she developed the theory and practice of material-based design computation. Prior to MIT, she received her diploma from the AA (RIBA 2) after attending the Faculty of Architecture and Town Planning at the Technion Israel Institute of Technology and the Department of Medical Sciences at the Hebrew University in Jerusalem. She has received numerous awards and her work has been exhibited widely and is part of the permanent collection of the Museum of Modern Art (MoMA) in New York and the Centre Pompidou in Paris.

Steffen Reichert is a research associate and doctoral candidate at the ICD at the University of Stuttgart. He received a master of science in design and computation (SMArchS) from the Massachusetts Institute of Technology (MIT) and a diploma with distinction in product design from the HFG-Offenbach. His research focuses on the relationship of the form, fabrication and performance of biologically inspired, responsive systems based on anisotropic material behaviour.

Simon Schleicher graduated from MIT with an MArch degree. He is currently working towards his PhD at the ITKE at the University of Stuttgart, which has its research focus on fibre-reinforced materials and bio-inspired elastic structures.

Hannes Schwertfeger studied architecture in Kassel, Delft, Mexico City and Stuttgart, where he was assistant professor at the IGMA. He is a founding member of the Baubotanik research group, and his PhD focuses on 'Fragile architecture and the aesthetics of the parlous'. He has been running the Bureau Baubotanik with Oliver Storz since 2010.

Tobias Schwinn studied architecture at the Bauhaus University in Weimar, Germany, and at the University of Pennsylvania in Philadelphia as part of the US-EU Joint Consortium for Higher Education. Prior to joining the ICD at the University of Stuttgart, he worked as a senior designer for Skidmore, Owings & Merrill LLP in New York and London with a special focus on computational design, complex geometry, automation and sustainability. He has been invited studio critic at Columbia Graduate School of Architecture, Planning and Preservation (GSAPP), Harvard University Graduate School of Design (GSD), Pratt Institute and the AA in London, and has taught various workshops on scripting and algorithmic design. His current focus is the integration of robotic fabrication with the computational design process.

Bob Sheil is a senior lecturer at the Bartlett School of Architecture, UCL, where he is Director of Technology and Computing,

and runs MArch Unit 23 with Emmanuel Vercruysse. He is a founding partner of sixteen*(makers) whose recent work in collaboration with Stahlbogen GmbH '55/02' won a RIBA award. He has edited two editions of *AD*: *Design through Making* (2005) and *Protoarchitecture* (2008). In 2011 he co-chaired the highly successful international conference 'FABRICATE' at UCL with Ruairi Glynn. In 2012 he will publish *Manufacturing the Bespoke*, an △ Reader on prototyping and making architecture in the digital age.

Rupert Soar is a director of Freeform Construction Ltd. He is a specialist in additive manufacturing and digital fabrication for construction. Freeform Construction acts as consultant and technology developer for new phase-changes materials, processes and applications ranging from novel partitioning, cladding and monocoque solutions to passive ventilation strategies based on termite mound impedance structures.

Oliver Storz studied architecture at the University of Stuttgart and TU Delft, and is a founding member of the Baubotanik research group. His PhD focuses on the constructive aspects of the baubotanik construction method. He has been running the Bureau Baubotanik with Hannes Schwertfeger since 2010.

Skylar Tibbits is a trained architect and computer scientist whose research focuses on developing self-assembly technologies for large-scale structures in our physical environment. He currently resides in Boston, Massachusetts, is the founder and principal of a multidisciplinary research-based practice, SJET LLC, and teaches at MIT's Architecture Department. He was recently awarded a 2012 TED Senior Fellowship and was named a Revolutionary Mind in *SEED* magazine's 2008 Design Issue. He has previously worked at a number of design offices including Zaha Hadid Architects, Asymptote Architecture, SKIII Space Variations and Point b Design. He has designed, collaborated and built large-scale installations around the world and exhibited at the Guggenheim Museum in New York and at the Beijing Biennale.

J Scott Turner is a professor of biology at the SUNY College of Environmental Science and Forestry in Syracuse, New York. He is the author of two books on the processes of adaptation and biological design: *The Extended Organism: The Physiology of Animal-Built Structures* (2000) and *The Tinkerer's Accomplice: How Design Emerges from Life Itself* (2007), both published by Harvard University Press.

Michael Weinstock is an architect, and currently a director of research and development, and director of the Emergent Technologies and Design (EmTech) programme at the AA in London. Over the last decade his published work has arisen from research into the dynamics, forms and energy transactions of natural systems, and the application of the mathematics and processes of emergence to cities, groups of buildings within cities and individual buildings. While his principal research and teaching has been conducted at the AA, he has published and lectured widely, and taught seminar courses, studios and workshops on these topics at many other schools of architecture in Europe and the US.

ABOUT ARCHITECTURAL DESIGN

INDIVIDUAL BACKLIST ISSUES OF △ ARE AVAILABLE FOR PURCHASE AT £22.99 / US$45

TO ORDER AND SUBSCRIBE SEE BELOW

What is Architectural Design?

Founded in 1930, *Architectural Design* (△) is an influential and prestigious publication. It combines the currency and topicality of a newsstand journal with the rigour and production qualities of a book. With an almost unrivalled reputation worldwide, it is consistently at the forefront of cultural thought and design.

Each title of △ is edited by an invited guest-editor, who is an international expert in the field. Renowned for being at the leading edge of design and new technologies, △ also covers themes as diverse as: architectural history, the environment, interior design, landscape architecture and urban design.

Provocative and inspirational, △ inspires theoretical, creative and technological advances. It questions the outcome of technical innovations as well as the far-reaching social, cultural and environmental challenges that present themselves today.

For further information on △, subscriptions and purchasing single issues see: www.architectural-design-magazine.com

How to Subscribe

With 6 issues a year, you can subscribe to △ (either print or online), or buy titles individually.

Subscribe today to receive 6 issues delivered direct to your door!

INSTITUTIONAL SUBSCRIPTION
£230 / US$431 combined print & online

INSTITUTIONAL SUBSCRIPTION
£200 / US$375 print or online

PERSONAL RATE SUBSCRIPTION
£120 / US$189 print only

STUDENT RATE SUBSCRIPTION
£75 / US$117 print only

To subscribe:
Tel: +44 (0) 1243 843272
Email: cs-journals@wiley.com

Volume 80 No 6
ISBN 978 0470 746622

Volume 81 No 1
ISBN 978 04707 47209

Volume 81 No 2
ISBN 978 0470 748282

Volume 81 No 3
ISBN 978 0470 664926

Volume 81 No 4
ISBN 978 0470 686806

Volume 81 No 5
ISBN 978 0470 669884

Volume 81 No 6
ISBN 978 0470 689790

Volume 82 No 1
ISBN 978 1119 993780